FOR I AM JOHN

For information address Soul Journeys/ Tony Barton, Nerang, Qld

ISBN 0-9580047-0-6

Printed in Australia
Published by
Soul Journeys, P.O. Box 367, Nerang, Queensland 4211, Australia

FOR I AM JOHN

By
Helen Barton

Published by Soul Journeys, P.O. Box 367, Nerang, Qld. 4211 Australia.

DEDICATION

This book is dedicated to all who are on the
journey of self-discovery:
To those who seek to know and understand in
order to help others:
To those Beings of Light and Love who assist
us all so patiently:
and finally to John whose infinite love and
guidance gave rise to this book.

ACKNOWLEDGMENTS

I wish to thank the very special people who assisted and supported me on this journey.

To my husband, Tony, who prodded and pushed, supported and encouraged and even took care of the household duties!

To my friend and colleague, Sherrie, who was prepared to listen and ask and then found she lived the teachings in the book. Perhaps next time we'll look at the fine print?

To Rex who took the time to encourage and nag me into action and then supported the whole work. You may have created a monster!

To Pop, Marina and Cynthia who gave their time at the end to ask further questions to amplify or clarify.

I could not have done this without their willingness to be in time with the project and to be there when needed. Everyone needs support and encouragement at some point and they offered it unconditionally.

My thanks and Love to you all.

Introduction

'For I am John' is a phrase, which always denotes the ending of the interaction for people who seek the guidance of this very wise and loving Being.

His purpose is to share a body of teaching and understanding with individuals and groups: to help them to move beyond the limitations of the personality and the soul and to find peace and joy. His channelled sessions with clients provide insights and understanding given with love, compassion and often a delightful humour.

He asked that we take the time to enable the information to be channelled since it is time for Humanity as a whole to begin to move forward. That this book would be the first of many building a body of teaching for all those who seek to 'know with the heart and love with the mind.'

I first connected with John as a baby and young child. He was as real to me then and now as are the members of my family. However, it was only after we emigrated from England to New Zealand that he reconnected once again. That was the period of my training and working with others. When we emigrated to Australia that intensified and then came the challenge of working overseas in Singapore, Hong Kong, Bali and Hawaii.

John now has many 'friends' around the world, some of whom have never met him in the flesh, so to speak. He asks that any questions, which may arise as you read this material, be directed to insight2@bigpond.com since he knows there will be another slimmer volume in response to these.

Chapter One
Belief and the Belief System

And we bid you welcome. We are going to have a very interesting time because we going to be discussing over a period of time many aspects of spirituality and physicality that need to be clearly understood in order that individuals may be able to move confidently along the path of their own progress and soul's purpose, do you see?

This is the introduction, if you will, to the material that we are going to supply to you. Many souls seek to develop themselves spiritually and, of course, that is the greatest illusion because they are already developed spiritually. They've just forgotten about it. And, as a consequence, there is much information presented in your world, which appears to be contradictory.

The purpose of this material is to attempt to simplify and to clarify so that those who choose to be reading it can create for themselves a foundation upon which they can build, do you see? Because if there is no foundation, they are going to fall over.

And so, we would request that this particular introduction is included so that there is an understanding of the purpose of this particular volume because there are going to be many more. Are you willing to do this?
Yes.
Then we thank you. Is always very good to have agreement, do you see?

And so, the first topic about which we are going to speak is a topic about belief and belief systems. Any individual who chooses to develop spiritually already has a belief system within them: whether it is conscious choice or whether it is as a consequence of their life and bringing up the belief system is already very active.

And so, in the desire to develop, there must be the overcoming of the old beliefs, the limiting beliefs, in order to move forward. For example, if you are having an experience, which suddenly causes you to ponder whether there is any survival after the death of the physical body and yet you have been raised among those who believe that the physical death is the final stage, nothing more, then there is a conflict, is there not?
Yes.
And as a consequence, either the individual is going to have to choose between one or the other or the individual is going to deny both until further information is available to make it possible to have a choice. Do you see?

In the deciding between one or the other, in the choosing of what it is that individual is now going to accept, there is a conflict and there is a guilt that is born within the individual. The guilt stems from the fact that, despite the upbringing, now there is a questioning of that old belief pattern. And so, therefore, as a consequence, there is a question of disloyalty, do you see?
Yes.

And that is very difficult for any individual, especially if they are trying to be spiritual because to be disloyal does not appear to apply to being spiritual. It is a very clever trap. Do you understand?
Mmm.
Is there clarity about what we have expressed because if

2

there is not we better begin to clarify a little bit more.

I think it could be put in more simple terms.

Then we will do so.

However, if we make it too simple, then those who are very intellectual are going to think, "Oh well, this is beneath who we be." So there must be the ability to be available to all degrees of intelligence, do you see?

Yes.

Therefore as a consequence we will give the simplified version.

You have an experience, which causes you to question a belief you have held all of your present lifetime. The moment you question the belief there is the introduction of guilt because you are feeling guilty for questioning a belief that has been given to you by those for whom you care and who care about you. And so, if you are questioning them, the guilt stems from whether they will believe that you no longer care about them. Do you see?

Yes.

And in the questioning, if you are verbally expressing what it is you are questioning, then you are going to feel disloyal that you are challenging a belief that has been shared with you for your good by those who care for you. Are they going to feel hurt? Because now you are not agreeing with them, you are challenging them. And for those individuals who are very strong in their sense of self, there will be the ability to move beyond it.

However, those who are not strong in their sense of self will have great difficulty with this aspect because emotionally they will be more focused upon not creating harm to others. Do you see?

Yes, very good.

Does this clarify?
Yes.
And as a final extension of this, even if they are willing to make the attempt, they are then in a situation where, by being disloyal, does this mean they are not being spiritual? Because surely, if you are a spiritual being, loyalty is very, very important.

So there is a trap that many in your world fall into because there is no clarity about it and because their emotional body is being activated. This must be so, to enable the growth and the expansion of the spiritual energy. Is this clear?
Yes. I do have a question.
Please to ask.
With loyalty, disloyalty and spirituality, the only person you have to be loyal to is yourself, is that correct?
That is so.
So disloyalty to someone else is only a perception?

However, it is the perception of the individual who is beginning to challenge, do you see?
Mmm.
It is a possible perception because not all individuals view it from this perspective. Those who have spent their lives seeking only to be of assistance to others, or do not have a strong sense of self or their own worthiness, are going to have great difficulty appearing to be disloyal when they are striving so hard to be spiritual. It creates within them a judgement. Those whom they are challenging may not see it in this light at all. However, that is not the concern. The individual will feel it.
Yes.
And so this creates within the individual a judgement of self and it is the judgment of self, not the disloyalty that creates

4

the barrier to the flow of the spiritual energy. Do you understand?
Yes.

Where the spiritual growth is concerned, loyalty to **the individual** is all tha˙ is of consequence. And that is a comment that will be challenged by many in your world. They will perceive it to be a statement to be self indulgent and self centred. That is quite a different kettle of your fish. In the context of which we are speaking, the loyalty to the individual is all important and yet, the majority of individuals will see themselves as being disloyal because they are even considering questioning.
And that feeling will be enhanced because the moment they begin to express to others, "This is what I am pondering," then these others, who perhaps have not had this kind of an experience or thought will ask them what is wrong with them; or will say, "Why are you stepping into such a situation?" Or will dismiss the question as being inappropriate. Because these ones are also answering from their own belief systems. Do you see?
Yes.

So therefore if you choosing to open yourself to the fullness of who you Be spiritually, it is very important to begin to examine the beliefs you hold about your God, whatever term you care to use for your God, about the ethics of being spiritual, about whether this is the only life you are able to be leading, about what you think you developing your spirituality for and to list all of these things upon your piece of paper.

Then, as you begin your journey, when the challenges to your old belief systems arise, as they always do, you are

5

not going to step into guilt because you already thought about it; and you have therefore moved beyond the emotion of it. Do you see? Do you understand?

Mmm.

Is it simple in its clarity for you?

I think it's .....I think it will be because when it's written, someone can go back and read that statement an infinite number of times.

That is so.

Whereas with the spoken word you only hear it the once and the moment is gone; but with the written word you can keep going back.

That is why this book is so important because it will provide the opportunity for many in your world to continually reassess, do you see?

Yes.

So if you have already thought about what are your belief systems, in thinking about it you are saying to your mind, "I wish to know what it is I believe." It is a conscious action, is it not?

Yes.

And so your mind will then begin to give to you examples of what your belief system is.

The obvious ones you will have no difficulty recognising and recording for yourself. However, what will occur is that during the course of a few weeks of your time, your subconscious beliefs will begin to rise to the surface because situations will develop that will enable you to recognise that you have these hidden beliefs also, do you see? So you are creating this because you wish to recognise and understand these beliefs.

When you have recorded each of them, it is beneficial then

to ask yourself where did this belief originate? You will either remember an event; you will remember a person that led you to this belief, or a teaching. And as a consequence, you will have an understanding of why you are holding that particular belief. That is very important because you have an understanding, as you begin to expand upon your spiritual sense of self; you will not feel guilty if you begin to understand in a wider sense than that which you have recorded. It becomes a mental exercise, not an emotional conflict.

You can compare what you are learning with what you have believed and as a consequence you can assess. "How does this fit into my belief system? Is it appropriate or does it replace my belief system because it makes more of a sense to me?" And because it is a mental exercise, then the emotional conflict will be allayed within you at that time. If there is a subconscious doubt, then you will create a situation where another individual will challenge the new attitude or belief you are holding, and as they do so and you answer, you will clear away your own doubt, do you see?
Mmm.
It is very important to examine beliefs. Because of beliefs and the systems, which derive from them, there has been much slaughter in your world. Beliefs have become so entrenched within the individual that they are no longer questioned with regard to spirituality, and certainly not with regard to unconditional love. Therefore there is much of limitation and blockage of growth. And yet to challenge a belief system is to be a heretic, is this not so?
Yes.

Well, think about it. The Master Teacher, Jesus, was a heretic

7

and look at the effect he had upon your world! He was educated as a Jew with the belief systems of Judaism. That was his upbringing. That was the belief system at the time of his incarnation and his training, his learning, his understanding. And yet, when he entered his synagogue to share with others the new understanding, he was asked to leave. Indeed, he was forcibly removed from this place by those who believed they had the only direct connection to your God, because they were not questioning or challenging the belief system at all. And so, as a consequence, he was considered a heretic.

Your Church, however, has never recognised this. The Church has said, "He is the Son of God." And when anybody questions the teaching of the Church, the Church does exactly what the synagogue did to the Master Teacher, Jesus. If the question or the challenge is so very strong that it could influence the minds and hearts of others, well this individual better be excommunicated, do you see? So the Church is repeating exactly what it is the Master Teacher, Jesus, strove to correct. And yet, there is so much belief, emotional fanaticism, attached to the religions of your day that they are not willing to recognise it. It is common sense when you think about it, do you see?

So many of the individuals of your world believe wholeheartedly. Their belief system gives to them a sense of comfort, a sense of security, particularly if their situation is very difficult or adverse. And yet their belief, if the trappings of your systems of belief were removed, would enable them to have a much clearer understanding of their God. The trappings of the belief system create these wars that are considered to be holy.

In actuality, the belief system has provided the perfect excuse for those who wish to be aggressive to do so because the moment you make it a Holy war, well, it must be perfect to be fighting it, do you see? The moment it becomes a Holy war, everybody says, "Oh well, we must be going to this place and fighting to the best of our ability. And if we die it matters not because we are assured that we going to go to God because it is God's war we are fighting."

And He's on my side?

Of course. So your God is a very clever fellow because He manages to be on everybody's side so therefore He must be fighting Himself. It is ridiculous, is it not?

Yes.

The Holy war is a beautiful tool because not only does it focus the attention of the people of a particular country outside of the difficulties of their lives, it also ensures that there is no more questioning of their religion.

Mmm. It takes them away from their inner.

If they are beginning to have doubt about their faith, if they are beginning to express criticism about how their country is being ruled, then this could be dangerous because as they voice what it is they are thinking and feeling, and understanding on a wider scale, others may be contaminated by it. If you persecute these ones, well you only going to add fuel to the fire of this dissent. Therefore, the simplest solution is, "We better look around, external to the country, where is there a situation where we can say, "Oh, this is against our God. This is persecution that must be addressed." And we better tell our people about this terrible persecution, because instantly if they know this is a Holy war, they going to forget about fighting internally and they going to rush to fight this war because that is their belief." Do you see? It is a very clever manipulation.

This is why we say, when you are beginning to open your mind to the possibility that there is more in your world than you have yet understood or recognised, it is very important that you list on your paper, so that you can review the beliefs that you know you are holding. And when you are learning something, accessing something, and you have a conflict about it, then you take this piece of paper and you look to see if this conflict has already been written upon this paper. If it has not, then you think about what is the area of conflict and so you recognise a subconscious belief. When you recognise within yourself a conflict about what it is you are becoming aware of; and if you look at your piece of paper and there is no such belief which appears to relate to your conflict; then you examine what is the area of the conflict and then you can understand what is the belief that you had not been recognising. And so, it remains a mental exercise because when you are dealing with understanding your belief systems, is no good being emotional about it because that is where the belief system gathers its power. Your religions are so very successful because they appeal to the emotional energy of your peoples. So, therefore, you're not wishing to change your belief by being emotional.

It is important to have the understanding of the belief, the understanding of the difference you are now introducing. Then you can assist yourself in moving through the emotional attachment without falling into guilt, do you see? That is the point, which we are intent upon emphasising.

Your belief system is your prison because once it is established within you, you never question it unless a situation arises which causes you to doubt or wonder; and

that is your guidance talking to you. It is saying to you, "Excuse me, you have been having a very beautiful sleep. Do you think is now time to be waking up, having a look at your world as it is in reality?"
Very good.
And so by examining your belief systems at the beginning of your development, you going to have less conflict as you move through it because you are already understanding where you have been limiting who you Be by that belief.

And because you have an understanding about it, you going to be happier about changing the limitation. Is why we say to you not to be converting any other individual because when you do so, you do so from the emotional body. You are enthusiastic, do you see?
Mmm.
And of course, your emotional body is going to activate the emotional body of the people you speaking to. And then this individual is either going to become cranky about what you saying, because it is clashing with what is their own belief system, or they going to say that yes it makes a tremendous amount of sense and they are going to do this. They have no understanding so when the challenge arises for them, your conversion fails because the old beliefs have not been recognised and addressed.

Your Jesuit teachers knew this many centuries ago; that your belief system is formed in the first seven years of your life. Everything else you experience confirms your belief. Is automatic because most of the time, you not even aware that that is what you believe in. And just because you not aware of it, does not mean that your mind is not going to continually create situations to affirm it. That is its work, do you see? And so, it will do so.

It is only when you present it with another piece of information, and it seems to be contradictory, or more expansive than what it is you have been knowing, that you have an opportunity to look at, to question and perhaps to change your beliefs. So do you understand why it is that we begin by talking about the belief system?
Yes.
Because that is the framework from which you begin to seek to actively develop. If you do not know what this framework is, how you going to know if it's big enough for what you doing? How you going to know if it's strong enough for what you doing?

Do you have any question about what it is we have been saying? Because then we can be amplifying a little bit more of the information.

I had one thought. You talked about loyalty and it's formed from the basis of a belief system. So people develop their morals from the belief system?

That is so.
Right.
If you think about it, it is why your morality changes because as your belief system changes, so your morality must change with it.
A lot of people stop at the moral and don't see the belief system behind it?
That is so.
Mmm, very good, because they have moral dilemmas.
Of course they do because they are confused that there are two beliefs within them that are clashing against each other; and so they think they have a moral dilemma. They do not.

12

They have a conflict about their beliefs. We give you a good example. Supposing the last life in which you incarnated was approximately 2,500 of your years ago. And you are incarnating in a civilisation where the bloodline of the rulers of the people was most important; needed to be maintained because the belief system of the day was that these rulers had special powers of contacting the Gods. And supposing they suddenly recognised that these families were getting very small, not enough people to be marrying into, to ensure the survival of this bloodline.

So what is introduced is that it makes sense therefore that the brother and the sister, or the father and the daughter, should thus marry to create children because the bloodline is being preserved, do you see? And so you are born into this period of time; and then suddenly you are born into this period of time **now**. You're going to have a difficulty, are you not? Because you have carried through a belief, that you are now ready to change; and because the belief systems of your world have already changed to make what was acceptable totally inappropriate. No allowance is made for the beliefs you incarnated with, that at a soul level you are now recognising are limiting: and so you choose your life circumstances and the religion, or the race or the creed into which you are born to enable you to question that belief, held at a soul level, and change it.

The past and the present thus combine and you create a new future.
Does this clarify for you?
Yes.
It is a long explanation, is it not?
No. It's very good.
Do you have another question?

Do you have another question?
I have a question about the format of the book.
Well, that is very appropriate. It's to do with belief systems also, is it not?
If that's what you believe, yes.
Think about it. Please to ask your question.

Is the book to be written…some books I've seen are like a question and answer? The way the book's written, it's like a question and we'll take the question Sherrie has asked. It's written like our weekly channellings are written. It's like a question and answer. Or do we not write it in that manner?

You going to combine. We going to present you first in each of these interactions with a body of material as we have done upon this occasion.
Mmm.
We are presenting you with the material itself and then we asking you do you wish to question anything about it? Because your questioning will also be included to show where aspects have been amplified. When the book is being sent out into your world you will find there will be people who will read the information, think about it, integrate it and they will have questions about it. And then they will make connection with you saying, "What about this question? Can you please clarify upon this subject?"

That is going to be another volume, do you see? Because by presenting the information to your world, you are planting seeds. When the questioning comes, and some will be quite critical, be prepared. There are going to be those who going to be very challenged, which is very good because it means that their belief system is very strong and they becoming aware of it. When the questioning comes to you, then you will produce a volume, which is purely question/answer, relating to each of the topics of this particular book. So your chapters will be about the same topics, simply question/answer.

It's not going to be a very thick book but will be an extension of this first one. There is one other thing we wish to be saying about this book. We are eavesdropping whilst you were talking about it with the others. You were having a discussion about how it is going to be presented, were you not?
Yes.
And you were wondering what kind of a colouring, what kind of a patterning, etc, etc. There is to be one cover for all of these volumes. And of course, you know what is the colour, do you not?
Yes. I believe we spoke about it.
You spoke about this blue colour.
Yes.
When you are preparing, consider the writing upon it, not to be gold, not to be silver but to be rose. Because both of these colours represent the soul/personality aspect of this energy of John, do you see?
O.K.
It does not mean you have to fulfil. We are asking you to consider and to experiment to see what it is appearing to be. The internal of the book, the writing internally, is to be blue. No question about it. You are speaking about the writing upon the cover of the volume, do you see?
Yes.
So does this answer your questioning about the content and how it is to be presented?
I think so.

Is there any other question you wish to be asking about

what we presented to you?
Will you be giving us the chapter headings? The title of each chapter?
Indeed, what do you think is the title of this particular chapter?
Belief and the Belief System?
That is so. We not going to be talking about individual beliefs, if they are in error, where they are in error. That is to be controversial. And there is no purpose to be achieved by it, do you see?
Indeed, yes.

So therefore we are talking about belief systems in general and not simply about your religion. If you have a belief that you going to be travelling to your moon, then everything you do will be as a consequence of moving into the position that will enable you to do so. If you have a belief that you are going to be completing your life at an early age, then you will create a disease that enables you to do so, or you will place yourself in a situation of accident where your life is ended. So this is why we say to you to examine the beliefs you hold about yourself, about your life, about your career and about your God. Because only through understanding what it is you believe about all these things, can you then hope to create a foundation that is solid enough for your development and growth, do you see?
Yes.
So that is why this is to be added to what we have already being saying about beliefs. Is there another question you wish to be asking about it?

When the book was first mentioned and a question arose about publishing the book, you mentioned that that would be taken care of.

That is so.
And that still applies?
That is so.
Good.
That is all we going to say about it, do you see?
Yes.
Because it's not yet time for you to know about it.
No. It's in the future.
That is so. And it is more important for the focus to be upon the actual preparation of it, than upon how you going to deliver it to your world. There have been suggestions you have been making about what you can be doing. And one thing we will say to you is that it's a very good idea to be your own publisher.
However, there are many ways of publishing for yourself, do you see?
Mmm.
So that is a clue. Is there any further question about beliefs or belief systems or do you believe we have given to you sufficient information for this chapter?

Well, just for clarity, you have used that people will think that they are disloyal. I feel that they could step out. From my own example, yes, disloyal is one but it's like 'that's the evil, devil'; it's used on a religious scale as well. All on a different scale. Is that the same energy?

That is so. Think about it. How was the Master Teacher, Jesus perceived? He was thrown out of the synagogue. He must be possessed of a devil for daring to be speaking this way. And then of course, he absolutely confirmed this belief because when he went to the Temple, he threw all of the tables over.

And this is then a big thing in the Bible too, that we are then sinners? Or keeps us in that, is it anything to do with that?
There is a confusion. We better clarify this. Your Bible is comprised of what is called the Old Testament and the New. Very interesting word testament because you are giving a testament about what is occurring and what is the belief, do you see?
Yes.

The Old Testament is based upon Judaism, the Jewish belief, and indeed there is a correspondence between Judaism and this Old Testament. The beliefs are the same because it deals with the Law and because during that period of your history, these people were very wild and very lawless. Not simply the Jewish people, but the people who lived in this area of your planet. They always having an invasion of each other, taking slaves, etc. etc. So when your people were released from the slavery and your Moses was given the Commandments, they were given as a system upon which to build a community, to build a life.

If you think about these Ten Commandments, they are based upon harmlessness.
Yes.
We going to talk about this at another time.

However, because these people knew only how to conquer or be defeated, the God had to be one who could conquer them if they misbehaved. He could cast them into Hell: He could strike them by lightening, do you see?
Mmm.
And so that is the belief system of this Old Testament. Is all based on fear: fear of this all-powerful God.

Your New Testament is based upon Love, on being unconditionally loving in your harmlessness. However, if you look at the belief system, it has been wonderfully converted, has it not?
Yes.
The unconditional love has been released and now, because they cannot use this angry God as a stick to beat you with, well, unless you worshipping this Master Teacher, Jesus, you going to Hell. Do you see? They have done exactly the same thing to the message. So when you are questioning, it is for you to decide. It is why we are making it a mental exercise.

Are you choosing to believe in a Being, a Supreme Being, of Unconditional Love? Or are you going to believe in a very vengeful kind of a creature who takes offence very, very easily because this is how this God is portrayed? If you go to your Church and you making too much noise within it, well your God is going to be striking you dead, unless of course you be singing to this God, in which case, he going to be very happy about it. Sounds a very limited creature, don't you think?
Yes.
Also very petty. That is because He has been fashioned from the minds of men, not from the message the Master Teacher, Jesus, delivered. Does this clarify for you?
Yes.

Of course, therefore, is not simply a belief system of the Christian people. The same applies with your Mohammed. He who came to teach that women were equal. Well, obviously he was very successful, was he not? Again the minds of men perverted the message. And your Buddha, the way of non-attachment, is this not so?

19

Mmm.

To be able to walk in peace and harmony with all concerned, knowing that it is appropriate. And so this is why those who are of Tibet are having a conflict with those who are of China.

Why?

They are not practising non-attachment. They are attaching to the place. There is continual activity trying to restore this place of Tibet to the people of Tibet. And yet their connection to their Buddha is not through a place. He taught this.

We could continue to enumerate all of the religions of the world and it makes no difference because it makes no difference. We not talking about religion specifically.

We are not saying that Buddhism is inaccurate; that Mohammed, and the Muslim faith, is inaccurate; Judaism, Christianity. That is not what we are saying.

We are saying that each of these religions delivered a very powerful and beautiful message to your world: and the minds of men created a belief system around the message that suffocated its Light. And unless you are able to examine and restore balance to your own belief system, at some point, no matter how far you think you moving spiritually, that belief system will cause you to fall over because you not addressed it.

Well, do you believe that we have now answered sufficient or do you wish that we be continuing because we quite happy to do so?

I feel that's as clear as it's going to be.

Yes, I feel that's clear.

That is very good. Then we say to you, we thank you for being part of this interaction, even though you did not be speaking much. There will be another. These interactions need to be as close together as is possible to do, because then the flow and the momentum of the energy can be seen by you. We do not have a problem with it because we know what it is. But if we be doing this close together, then as one flows from the other you will begin to see the pattern of the book forming. You will begin to understand why we are choosing to begin as we have done. And so your questioning will become very direct and focused as a consequence, do you see?

Yes.

Does this clarify for you?

Yes.

Then we thank you and we leave you with our blessing and our love.

Thank you.

Until we meet again.

For I am John.

Notes.

Notes.

Chapter Two
Understanding

And we bid you welcome. It is a pleasure to be able to be continuing with the information that is going to be creating this particular volume.

In our last discussion we were talking about belief systems and how they have an impact upon the individual, is this not so?
That's correct.
And, as a consequence, there is an understanding given in that information to facilitate those who cannot comprehend why others cannot understand. That is the greatest cause of conflict and aggression. If you can understand why there is a difference of belief, why both believe themselves to be accurate, then you can understand and avert a conflict.
So therefore, this second aspect of our teaching is about understanding, do you see?
Mmm. Yes.

First of all, you have a belief. No matter the belief, it does not have to be as a consequence of your spiritual development, can be to do with your physical day-to-day situation. That belief as we have already stated is the motivating factor in the life of the individual. If there is no understanding, either of the belief itself or the reason why the belief is present, then that individual operates unconsciously and reactively in your world, do you see?
Yes.
If, however, there is an understanding of why the belief is present, and indeed of the extent of the belief, then the individual is able to be responsive in your world, which is

why we were saying to make a list of your beliefs, and to contemplate when you acquired them, what were the circumstances, etc. etc., do you see?
Yes.
Because then you are becoming responsive rather than reactive and with regard to your spiritual progress that is a condition greatly to be desired because then you are working in partnership, do you see?
Yes.

Rather than being an individual blind to what is occurring or even to where the individual is going. Understanding covers many explanations and definitions. Indeed, language itself is open to many interpretations according to the nuances and intonations placed upon certain words in the vocabulary. And this is irrespective of what language it may be. Do you see?
Yes.
To have an understanding of your belief system is to be fully conscious of why you are holding this belief system, what you intending it to assist you to achieve and therefore how you are choosing to function in your world.

First of all, the understanding itself requires a lack of judgment. You cannot judge and be understanding. The two are mutually exclusive. Do you understand this?
Absolutely.
So in understanding you are removing the judgment of your belief system, which then enables you to expand upon what it is you are using as your structure or your system, do you see?
Mmm.
It enables you to change its shape, its form. It enables you to remove aspects of it, which are no longer valid for you,

and to build upon other aspects. This is called evolution. Do you understand?

I do. Can I ask you to wait for a moment? (Sherrie joins the session.)
Thank you. Please continue.

There is a tardiness, is there not?
Much traffic today.
And therefore no allowances made for the conditions, which is very appropriate with regard to what we are saying about understanding, do you see?
Mmm.
So we thank you because that is a perfect example of what it is we are discussing. If you understand a situation, in this case we talking about your belief system, if you understand your belief system and why it's present then you are able to make allowances in it for any circumstance. Do you understand this?
Yes, I think so.
If you know that you believe a particular thing then you going to be aware that not every individual in your world is going to believe it as you do. This is so, is it not?
Yes.
Your belief is personal to you. If you choose to be responsive in your world, well then you better think about what are the possible outcomes of the expression of this belief.

There are going to be those who say that it is very interesting, however, they are not interested in it. There are going to be those who say that it is not so very wonderful and wonder what it is you are really saying. And there are going to be those who say that it is absolutely untrue because it does not fall into alignment with their own belief system.

Therefore, if you are understanding that these are possible outcomes of your beliefs, you can then work within yourself so that you can be responsive in all of these situations rather than reactive. Does this clarify?

Yes.

If you know an individual is going to deny the truth of what it is you are believing, it is because you have understood that your belief and the individual's belief are not the same. Is this not so?

Yes.

Therefore, if you know, if you understand that where you are standing is in a different position to this other individual, if you are aware of this before you choose to step forward, there is no possible reason for reaction to what it is this other is denying, do you see? Is this clear?

I think it could be clearer, perhaps in more simple terms.

We give an example. Supposing that you believe your world is round and you are living in a time where the belief is that the world is flat, because this actually occurred in your history, did it not?

So therefore there are many people walking about the place believing that if they go too far they going to fall off. And there are others who are beginning to understand that no matter how far they walk, they simply going to continue until they come back to the place from whence they began; and therefore no falling off is possible.

If you know, as your own belief, that your world is round and you know that others do not agree with you, when you are talking about it with an individual who believes it is flat, and this individual says to you, "You are totally wrong. This is the truth of the matter." If you have an understanding of

why your belief is there, you are not going to be reactive to what is being expressed. You will understand that this individual is expressing his truth and reacting to what you are saying. Do you see?
Yes.
So this individual is fearful because you are proposing something that is beyond his knowing. Of course, he is going to be denying it. It is a natural reaction, is it not?
Mmm.
If you understand this, then when this one says, "No, No. You are very wrong", you are going to say, "Well, I am simply sharing my truth with you" and you walk away.

If you do not understand your own belief system or make allowances for the differences of opinion of others, when this individual denies your belief, you going to go to war; because you have to prove who is right, who is wrong. It is a reaction, do you see? You are allowing this one's disbelief, fear and anger to be a catalyst for what lies within you that you are not understanding about your beliefs and why they are present. Because if you do not know why you believe a thing, well then, you are going to feel to a certain degree, powerless, are you not?
Yes.
So when another individual says that you are wrong, that is also saying to you that you are powerless. And you cannot be at peace within yourself because you do not understand why the belief is present within you. Do you see?
Mmm.

If you understand, "This is what I believe and this is why I believe it" you are at peace. And as a consequence, it enables you therefore to be open to the attitudes and truths of others; to be willing to listen to them without feeling fearful

27

that what they going to say might overset your own beliefs. Rather you going to listen from the perspective that what is said might enhance or expand your belief; give to you another perception of your truth that you may examine and decide whether you going to keep it or leave it alone.

So, therefore, understanding is tremendously important in your world. Where there is belief without understanding there is conflict. If you look at the history of your world, if you look at all of the wars that are fought, each war is fought about a belief system - not necessarily about a religion, but about a belief system, do you see?
Mmm.
And the war is fought because neither makes any attempt to understand the belief of the other, or even to understand why their own belief is present and how that belief may have an adverse impact upon others. No allowance is made for this. There is an arrogance.
"This is my belief. I am accurate. Therefore, you either accept it or I going to go to war with you. And because my belief is so accurate, obviously I am highly civilised, highly evolved human being and you are not. So I have to teach you how to be so." Do you see?

That is called civilisation. And yet, it is a most uncivilised manner of interacting one to another; because without understanding there can be no respect; and if there is no respect, there is no honour either of your own belief or the belief of another. There is simply enforcement.

And so, tardiness is an outcome of a belief, do you see? We going to use this as an example because it has nothing to do with spirituality. Do you understand?
Oh, yes.

28

If you tardy in what it is you doing, is because you believe you have plenty of your time to be doing whatever it is you wish to be doing. Is this not so?

Mmm.

"I going to do this. It's going to take this amount of my time and so everything going to be in perfect alignment." Which is very wonderful when everything is flowing perfectly. Do you see?

Yes.

However, if the conditions have changed, then the timing is going to be influenced, do you see?

Yes.

And it is when there is no allowance made because the understanding is not present about the circumstances, that belief systems create chaos and ultimately aggression. Do you see?

Mmm. Yes.

So that is a very simple example.

I can relate to it today.

Very good: because it enables you then to have clarity about it, do you see?

And if you follow it to another extreme, just supposing you are the Prime Minister of your country. You are having this meeting with the Prime Minister of another country and you going to be discussing mutual cooperation. So, is a very important meeting, do you see?

Each of you is going to be talking to each other. Each of you looking for what benefits you can be achieving for yourselves. And there is a tardiness at arriving, do you see? If no allowance has been made for the circumstances or conditions and one, in this case we going to say you, because we talking about you as the Prime Minister, you are late because somebody decided to have a accident in the middle of the road you are using. You did not know about it because it only just occurred and you are unable to be diverted to avoid it. So therefore you stuck.

When you arrive at this meeting, even though your apologies have been given to this individual, the atmosphere between you very chilly. Because this individual is saying to himself, "Well, I am a person of consequence. I have come here genuinely in search of mutual benefits and, even at the very beginning, before we are speaking, there is this slight given to me. If this one was truly sincere about having this meeting, there would have been sufficient time allowed in case anyone decided to have a accidental situation. This is a power play. This one is deliberately arriving late to show that she believe that she more powerful than am I." Do you see?
Mmm.

And because this is not spoken, the other one, in this case you, does not know this is the underlying attitude. So the meeting begins on a chilly note with a lack of understanding by both. Do you see?
Yes.
As a consequence, when the time comes to be making concessions, the one who has felt slighted is now determined to make as few concessions as possible but to obtain as many from you as possible so that this one can be saying that you not as powerful as you thought you were.

Oh God... That's really... Yes.... I do it all the time.

Now we have given this as an example that is going to be seen as highly exaggerated. However, every action and interaction in which you are involved is a meeting of two people who are the Prime Ministers of their world. Who believe themselves to be people of character, integrity and understanding. So therefore they going to take offence if the other one appears to be showing a lack of respect. And, if you have an understanding of this, and you apply it to all of your interactions, what do you think is going to occur? (*Pause.*) Obviously nothing.

No, I think that a lot of negativity is going to be directed back towards you from different people, from different sources. Your life will not flow.

You are not making allowance, because you not understanding where the other individual is: where <u>any</u> individual is. Do you see? However, if you have the understanding of it, then you are not going to create these kinds of circumstances or if you do because it is meant to be, your guidance has stepped in and created it: you must not forget that you have these lessons to be learning. If indeed it does occur, the moment you are meeting and there is a sense of chilliness, you can say. "Oh, I know exactly what this individual believes. I can understand why this individual is believing this. Therefore before we go any further in our interaction, it is important that I address this issue and take away the negative impression that has been generated." Do you see?
Mmm.

Does not mean that you have to be crawling about on the floor in abasement. Simply means that you express to this one. "This is what occurred. I am very sorry about it because I can appreciate that you are feeling slighted by this. (whatever term you feel suitable from the circumstance; we

are simply using the term from the example given.)
I can understand that you feel that I have shown you a lack
of respect in not honouring that who you Be and your time
is equally as important as my own." Do you see?
Yes.

You have addressed the issue through your understanding.
If the other one chooses not to accept what it is you are
saying, that is their learning. You, however, have cleared
the energy. It cannot attach to you as a negative because
you are not unconscious of your actions. You are
understanding the impact of them and taking responsibility
for it, do you see? And if there is an understanding, and if
there is a willingness to take responsibility, well, you going
to be quite amazed at what occurs in your world; because
at this point of your time everybody trying to give
responsibility to everybody else.
"This is not working because is your fault. This is not
happening because you not doing what you supposed to
be doing." No understanding, do you see?
Mmm.
A judgment, a criticism, well obviously this one then going
to punch you on the nose.

So do you understand, and this is no pun intended, what it
is we are saying about needing to have an understanding
of your belief system and why it is present? Because if you
do not understand why you believe what you do, then you're
not going to understand why others cannot accept your
beliefs.

So how does it feel to be Prime Minister? Is very good, is it
not?
(Laughter.) There's a lot of responsibility there.

Of course! However, you going to claim all of it very happily, are you not?

Yes.

Very good! Is there a question?

So, the understanding that one has of someone else is an unconditional acceptance of their belief system, as opposed to a judgment? Not an unconditional agreement, an unconditional acceptance.

We will clarify the wording a little bit more. You are almost accurate.

Almost?

Almost. Very well, are you ready for this explanation to be beginning?

Almost.

Very good, is very clever. If you have an understanding of your own belief system, then you have an unconditional acceptance of it because you know why you believe it. This is so, is it not?

Yes.

Therefore when you talking to another individual who is expressing their belief system, because you have no hidden areas within your own, you going to be able to have an unconditional acceptance of their right to have their belief system: not necessarily an unconditional acceptance of their belief system, because you might not agree with it. What you are unconditionally accepting is their right to have it. So that is why we say you almost accurate because you missed out the <u>right to have</u> their belief system.

I had to leave that for you.

Indeed you did, otherwise we would have had nothing to be saying, do you see?

(Laughter.) It would have been a very short chapter.

Very, very short! So does this clarify for you?
Mmm. It's the unconditional acceptance of that person's right to have an opinion, whatever that opinion may be. Yes, I can see the difference.

Because if you can accept the right of every individual then you not going to take it personally, automatically take it personally, if this individual does not share your own belief. You may think, "Oh, what a pity, such a nice individual to be so misguided," because you are so absolutely certain about your own. But you not going to say, "This individual is a fool. I better go to war, defeat this individual so that he may see the error of his ways and follow the <u>only</u> truth, which is **my** truth."

And we not simply speaking about your violence. The moment you seek to convert another you are going to war with them. The moment you seek to convert another, you are demonstrating your total lack of understanding for why they are choosing to believe what it is they are believing: your total lack of respect for the value they place upon their beliefs: and as a consequence a total dishonouring of their beliefs and your own.

Because, in order to convert, you have to prove this individual is wrong; that his belief is insufficient, inappropriate, incomplete in some manner; or, the most perfect of all statements, uncivilised. "Oh well, these individuals have these beliefs because they savages. They do not know any better, so we better teach them what is the most appropriate, because then they can be civilised, as are we." What arrogance!

What total contempt for these others because there was no

<u>attempt</u> to understand. And so, therefore, there could only be war. There could only be one defeated: rather than a coming together in harmony where all could learn from each other. Do you see?

But that's been the problem with mankind throughout modern history. If you look at the Native American Indians, the Southern American Indians, like the Aztecs, Incas, the same has happened to them.

Not simply your modern history. Has always been where one culture, one religion, one people chooses to convert another to their way of life; not even necessarily their belief system of religion, although that is the most common method of initiating this kind of a situation. Indeed, that is so. However, at various points throughout your history, the teachers that have come have come to say to you, "Stop a moment and please try to think. Understand who you be, where you be, where you going and what you doing as a consequence."

And so, we are simply reiterating this message again at this point of your time, because you still not understanding, do you see? So, every time there is a teacher come to impart this wisdom to your peoples, to your world, always there is a message about understanding. And it is quite amazing how very good your people are at ignoring this message. If you think about it, we going to use your Bible as a very good example, when your Moses was given the Ten Commandments, they were about harmlessness, were they not?
Mmm.

Because the people did not understand that they were about

harmlessness, they interpreted them as being absolutely literally engraved in stone. Do you see? "Oh, we better follow them because if we do not follow them, we going to get punished." There was no attempt made to understand why these commandments were given. And even your Moses was not able to fully understand it for himself, so therefore he could not explain it to your people. He tried to do so. Gradually, however, they were forgotten about.

"It's too difficult." It was too difficult because there was no understanding of why these commandments were necessarily given. And so, the people went into a reaction, which of course then enabled them to be suffering all of the trials and tribulations that they were suffering.

The Master Teacher, Jesus, taught about Love, harmlessness through Love. And He also sought to teach understanding. If you look at the teachings, if you look at the answers He gave when He was questioned, He was seeking to bring an understanding of what was occurring. So was your Buddha, so was Mohammed, etc., etc., etc., do you see?

And each time, a piece of the information was taken. A belief system was built around it and the understanding of that piece *as part of the whole* was missed or deliberately ignored.

So, you have thousands of people in your world who believe, most definitely.

However, if you were to ask them to help you to understand why they have this belief, they could not tell you. They believe because that is what they have been taught to do without being given the understanding of why it is important for them to have such a belief. And without understanding, your belief becomes a prison. Do you see?

Mmm.

So now you see why it is so very important to have an understanding of situations, do you not? Do you have a question? We hope you going to have many questions about it.

If you have a belief system without the understanding, it's not really a belief system, is it? Not a true belief system, more you're living your life according to someone else's belief system.

It is a true belief system; make no mistake about it. However, you are accurate. It is not <u>your</u> belief system. You are living in someone else's belief system because you do not understand why that belief is so important. It is why we say to you, when we talking about beliefs, to list what are your beliefs, to understand when you acquired them, how you acquired them, why you acquired them. Because then you going to see which are your own, as a consequence of your experiences, and which are beliefs you have adopted, as a consequence of your environment. Do you see?

Would it also be a good idea to put down one's old belief system and one's present day belief system? Because I know, for me personally, the belief system that I lived by 15 – 20 years ago isn't the same as today because I have a different understanding. Whether it's right or not, there's no judgment on it, it's just different. How I see life is different today than I did 10 years ago. So would it be interesting to write as it was and as it is?

It would serve more than one purpose. First of all, it would be beneficial because you would see the evolution of your own growth.

Indeed, yes.

Because you see where you began. You see where you are now.

"Oh, well. I have moved. I am not the same person even though I feel as though I am the same as I have always been." Do you see? Because how often do you stop and understand who you are now, in light of who you have been? The world is so very busy unless something occurs to make you do so, you do not do so. So is important from that perspective.

It is also important because if you look at your old belief and your current belief, and you are willing to understand how you moved from one to the other, in some circumstances you are going to see that although the focus of the belief may have changed, the need behind it remains the same. So therefore you can see where you have genuinely evolved and grown, and where you have simply exchanged one belief for another, which keeps you exactly where you were. You simply placed a different label upon it. Is a very positive exercise and will give to you quite a few surprises, do you see?

Yes.

You will discover certain things that you have not anticipated. However, you will also be able to congratulate yourself because you have grown. You have moved forward. You cannot live in your physical world and not have growth, do you see? Even when you appear to be standing still, you are growing.

Well, we have all grown because we are now Prime Ministers of our own world.

That is so. Your world is peopled by all of these Prime Ministers. And it is a very good term, Prime Minister. Prime because it is the number one and Minister because you ministering to your own needs. You not expecting somebody else to do it for you. Well, you may expect. However, is not going to happen.

The moment you take responsibility you going to do it for yourself. So understanding is of tremendous importance because if you not willing to understand, you going to repeat the pattern time after time after time. It is why, when you having a lesson you not particularly enjoying, you are asked to look for the gift within it. The gift is the understanding of what has occurred and why because, once you have the understanding, you do not need to repeat the situation, do you see?

And there's always that gift of understanding, if you willing to find it. And, in order to find it, it is important you suspend judgment of the circumstances or the situation or the belief. Because whilst ever you have judgment you cannot have understanding, do you see?
Mmm.
Do you have another question?

Could you give an explanation for myself and others who read this about belief systems and start to question and understand how they can recognise what is a belief? Because you can have beliefs and you can have an attitude. How do you recognise?

An attitude – this is why we say look at your beliefs and how you acquired them. Because in looking at your beliefs then you going to understand what is a belief and what is an attitude.

An attitude is something you have learned, do you see? A belief simply is. And, in the initial understanding, you look at your belief. You may not understand it. You simply know that you do. And it matters not what another says to you about it, you going to refute it. For example, we say to you your world is flat. What you going to say?
No, it's not.
How do you know is not?
Because I've been taught that.
How do you know is not flat? It's not because you been taught it or the information was given to you. You believe it to be round because you seen it with your own eyes.
Yes.
So if we say to you, "Sorry, your imaging is totally inaccurate. It's actually very square and is tumbling about in space as a cube, not as a ball." What you going to do?
Mmm. I'm going to say no because I've seen it.
And so, because you have seen it you believe it to be true.
Yes.
It is a belief, not an attitude. Because, if it was an attitude, and we were saying to you it's actually square, you would say, "Can you prove it? How do you come to such an understanding?"
Both of you said, "No, it's not." You did not even say, "Why do you think it's square?" You said, "No, it's not." Do you see?
Yes.
That is a belief. "No, is not." Or "Yes, it is."

O.K. so I had a thought as well, at the same time I was saying no, that O.K. we do see things illusionary. We have those pictures where we look at something one way and then you can see it's something else.

However, now you are in your head. And when you are in your head that is attitude.
O.K. great.
When you are in your belief, your belief stems from your emotional body. It is an instinctive reaction or response in any given circumstance. So, your instinctive reaction was, "No, is not." That was your belief system speaking.

However, your mind, with its attitude said, "Perhaps we could explore this because this could be an illusion. How do we know what is, what is not?"
(Laughs.) That's right, too.
So sometimes you can be expressing a belief whilst at the same time your mind is playing about with the idea of the belief.
Mmm.
No wonder you so confused, do you see?
Yes.
You will literally die for a belief. You will not die for an attitude. You will change your attitude. For example, we going to use a example of children because children always stir up everybody's beliefs. Is quite amazing.

So you are in a busy, busy area and there are some children around you. And you see one of the children about to be running in front of a very fast moving vehicle. And you are close to this one. Are you going to stand and watch it occur?
No. Your first response would be to run and push it out of the way.
Because you believe the child's life is more important than your own, do you see?

Mmm.

Because you are older and the child still has a life to live. So your belief says, "Perhaps I can save this one and any damage to myself is incidental."

The attitude could be, "Oh well. Logically, I'm not going to get there in time and I going to be injured for no purpose." The attitude does not have any impression in such a situation. Do you see?

Yes, I do.

And if you knew that in order to do something you might have to pay a penalty, but you believed in what you were doing, you would quite happily be willing to pay the penalty. That is a belief. Do you see? Whereas an attitude could say, "Oh well. I better go think about this. Perhaps I better not be paying this penalty. Perhaps I am in error."

With a belief, there is no doubt. That is why your reaction or response is instinctive. And it is why we say to you to please take the time to understand your beliefs: because when you understand them, you are going to be responsive in your world and responsible. And you may even find that you are holding certain beliefs that you now have a contrary belief about; you simply have not let go of the old. So then you can let it go and not going to be any fighting about it. It's why it's a good exercise to look at the past belief and the current belief, do you see?

Mmm.

Does this clarify for you?

Yes, it does. Very good, thank you because I've felt the experience happening in me in the way you've answered the question. Very good.

42

So, giving to you the understanding enables you to move forward, do you see?

Yes.

Is why understanding is so very important. Do you know why we are holding this? *(A crystal, which I hold during each session.)*

For Helen. Helen holds it.

Because the channel wants to.

Because the channel has a belief, do you see?

Yes.

And yet, when this channel is operating in your group environment, this is not present.

No.

Do you see? It is a belief, not an attitude. If it were an attitude, she would ensure that she had it with her at all times or not at all because she would see the contradiction of it. It is unconscious. It is simply automatic that when she in this kind of a situation this is what she is holding. Has no impact upon how well we going to work through her; and because part of her also believes that if she holding something like this she not going to be able to move.

Well, do you see, we going to place this in this position because it's not needed. Has not prevented us from moving and is not going to save her. She going to have much fun when she hears this. *(A reference to my resistance of John's ability to make my body move around.)*

However, please to ask your question.

I'll have to keep it brief because time is running out now. The instance you quoted with the child running in front of the car, and the immediate reaction for a lot of people would be to jump, to run, to try and save the child without any

43

consideration of their own welfare. If you were to stop and look and come to the conclusion that you couldn't save the child without injury to yourself, and then you realised that it was that child's karma, destiny, lesson, whatever you want to call it, to be there at that time, in front of that car; then by you jumping in front of it and saving it basically you are interfering with their karmic free will.

That is absolutely accurate. However, a belief system does not take the time to reason it out. Therefore, if you wish to discard that kind of a belief, first of all you have to understand that you hold it, why you hold it and then you are replacing it with this other. Is what we have been saying, do you see? So you replace the one with the other.
But in the situation itself, if you do not have that awareness, you going to instinctively react because you are taught from little, little children to sacrifice yourselves for others. Do you see?
I think that's silly.
Of course it's silly. However, it's a very wonderful way of controlling the numbers of your population because if you taught to sacrifice yourself for others, every time there is a conflict, you going to volunteer because you believe you doing good, do you see?
Yes. Absolutely.

So therefore your Prime Ministers never have a problem having people to go fight for them. However, do you notice they do not go fight themselves? Do you not find this quite ridiculous? Your government people are quite happy to create this war situation because they know they do not have to be going and fighting it. They may have already fought another in their progress to being in this government situation.

44

However, they have not learned from it. Because if they had learned the lesson from being in this fighting situation, when they achieved the power themselves, they would do everything in their power to make sure it never happens again. And they do not because they have no desire to understand the beliefs of the other. Their desire is simply to compel obedience to their own beliefs. Do you understand?
Mmm.

Without understanding your world cannot heal: because without understanding you cannot be unconditionally loving. Do you see?
Yes.
It is most important that you understand why you are believing as you are, and to be willing to understand why others choose to have a different belief. Because that is honour. That is seeing the God in every individual, rather than only seeing the God in yourself and everybody else has still to find this God and you going to be the only one that is going to enable them to do so. And if you have to punish them in order for this God to be born within them, if you have to kill them in order for this God to be born within them, well, that is absolutely perfect. Which in itself is a ridiculous statement because if you killed them, they are dead. How can the God within them take form in your world and have a impact?
There's no understanding. In such a situation there is only a belief that whatever the outcome, the action is necessary. Do you see?
Mmm.

So, we being quite forceful about it do you see? Because it is the lack of understanding that is at the root of **all** of the difficulties in your world at this time. And even more

45

importantly, it is the lack of the willingness to understand. And so, that is all we going to say about it.

We are quite aware of your time passing by quite quickly, so we are going to say to you we are completing this portion of what it is we have to be saying to you. There may be another part to it at a later time. We have laid the seeds for what is to come, do you see?

And so we thank you and we leave you.

For I am John

Notes.

Notes.

Chapter Three
Perception.

We bid you welcome. Now where to begin? Perception is a wonderful thing.

A beginning to an ending.

Indeed, because if there is no beginning therefore there cannot be an ending. How the dickens are you going to have one? Well you not, are you?

No.

Very good. For a moment there we thought you might be confused about it do you see? Now, we have to begin.

A beginning of a perception?

You cannot have a beginning of a perception because for you to begin to recognize, it is already there.

OK.

So it has actually been sneaking up upon you before you realized it, and when you beginning to realize it you already got it. So then you have to learn to understand it and be working with it, do you see? Well of course that is when the problem begins, is it not?

When potential misunderstanding rears it head.

Very good way of putting it because that is exactly what it is, a rearing of the head of a misuse potentially of a perception that in actual fact has been based upon the subconscious perception of events initially. Do you see?

I have to listen again, but I get the gist.

Because for you to recognize you got this perception you already been subconsciously assessing, evaluating, trying to be understanding, observing. Do you see?

Mmm.

So therefore your perception in that period is already giving rise to the perception you become aware of later. Does this clarify?

OK.

Very good, just one moment, we have to be thinking.

This is a very good idea, do you do this? *(He put his finger to the underside of the nostrils).* Do you do this?

Oh, yes, sometimes.

Do you know why you do it?

No.

It is because it is assisting your discrimination.

Oh.

Think about it.

Now, perception is a situation greatly to be understood and it is not at all understood in your world because it is dismissed. Do you understand?

Mmm.

People are saying to each other, 'well it is just your perception.'

Right, OK.

It is a discounting, do you see? Well how can you discount a perception? It is very important, otherwise why would you have it? It is giving to you some information, kind of a data situation, to enable you to begin to expand your energy.

OK, yes.

However, this is very important, when someone says to you, "Well that is just your perception," do you know what occurs? Your energy closes in.

Mmm. Because it is like a criticism.

Of course. What they are saying is that is your perception and your perception has no value. Because they are not saying to you, "Thank you very much for sharing this kind of

a situation." They are dismissive. So the moment you dismiss a perception you are closing down the individual.
OK.
So now we are understanding each other. We both having the same perception about this conversation, do you see?
Yes.

Very good! Point number two. This is also of significance. Now, perceptions come as a consequence of a questioning or an enhancing of a belief system.
If you are getting a perception that is contrary to your belief system, well you have a conflict. Because you on the one hand saying, "But I already believe this to be so." On the other hand you are saying, "How can this be so because of this?"
Yes.
So it is an opportunity for expansion.
Right.
If you have a blind kind of a belief you going to dismiss your own perception.
Oh yes, OK. Yes.
If your belief is based upon what you believe to be reason or understanding then this perception you are going to take to pieces to see how it can be fitting into this belief system.
OK. Yes, I get it.
If you are doing this then your belief system is growing, is alive, is open.

If however you have this kind of a perception, you try to place it into this belief system; it appears to be comfortable to you because it is just adding a little bit more meat to it, if you will. And then another individual says to you, "You cannot incorporate this into this." They are dismissing both your belief and your perception.

OK. Yes, double whammy.

Indeed, because your belief is allowing you to incorporate the two. So what they are saying to you is you got the wrong belief to begin with otherwise you would not be allowing this perception to be added to it.
Oh, I get it.
So basically what they are saying to you is that you actually been building your life on a misunderstanding of a belief, because if you understood it properly you would not be allowing this to be part of it.
Right.
So, what are you going to do about it?
Retreat.

Indeed, and that is exactly what occurs in your world. Your people pull away because they are confused, and more importantly they believe themselves to be judged. Which indeed they are. Now, with regard to the energy of the group whom you been working together... There was a change of the energy when you came together.
Yes.

Now you have been given a explanation for it, condensed kind of a version with this group member. That is a very good kind of a condensation and is important because it allows each of you then to take this matter to see what is your perception of it.
OK.
To see how you can incorporate it into your belief about what you doing, if indeed you going to do so, because you may decide it is a very interesting kind of a statement but not relevant. Do you see? It does not alter the fact that the energy of the group is changing.

OK.

As a consequence of the changing of the energy the perception of every individual in it is also going to change.
Yes, that makes sense.

So now what are you going to do? Because now you got this group of individuals who had come together, started to think they were thinking alike, sharing a common belief, common perception of their role. And now, because the energy is different, they have to go away and think about it all over again; and now what you have got is a situation where each individual's perception will be voiced and others may say, "Well yes, I can quite see that" or "No that does not make any kind of a sense, cannot therefore be so."
Mmm.

Do you see? You are not simply going to get agreement or disagreement. Because of the very nature of the group you are going to get a statement about it. Do you understand?
I think I will understand better when I hear the tape.

Very good. So for example you may say, "Well I have been listening to this information. My perception of the situation now is that suddenly we have gone up this ladder and at this point of this ladder we have to be getting off, waiting to do some more work before we are going anywhere else."
Right.

Someone else in the group may say to you, "But that is only your perception because my understanding is that from this point we can do everything we need to do." Well, you are going to feel closed down.
Yes.

And you are going to think to yourself it is a valid perception. Why is it mine is only a perception and this other fellow's is accurate? Who determines, do you see?
Yes.

53

So then you got a conflict.

Yes.

So where the group as a whole has been working together, well suddenly everybody going to be putting into the middle what they think and determining who is accurate, who is not accurate. You are going to have a very discombobulated energy. Which is absolutely wonderful. Do you see?

Yes.

Because now you are moving. Now you are growing again. Very good! Now, you got this energy, it is beginning to be expanding, you not quite certain what you are going to do with it.

Me personally?

You personally now, we are talking to you. You not quite certain what you are going to do with it, are you?

No.

Well that is very good, because then you cannot limit it. Do you see?

Mmm.

However, as you are exploring it, you going to find that you going to be getting ideas and concepts coming, flooding into your Being, not in any kind of an order.

Yes.

It is called random chaos. And you going to try, because you liking the detail very much, to fit them all into the correct placing. And it is going to be very exasperating for you because they are not going to fit. So the more you try to put them into this kind of a situation the less it is going to work.

OK.

What you got to do is you got to make a list of them. So as they are coming to you just be writing your note about it. Do not try to comprehend the fullness of it and do not try to make one follow on from another. Because then all your hair is going to fall out! Do you see? Not a good idea.

As a consequence, you going to be having all of this coming to you. You going to go to your group situation, no, we are missing out a step, wait a moment, because it is very important that you understand the significance of this.

You having all of this information coming in to you. At the same time your partner is having his fine little fencing game occurring with this Dweller fellow, do you see? (Here John is referring to the Dweller on the Threshold.)

He is quite accurate about it you know. However, this Dweller fellow is going to have fun with him. So he is going to be playing in this kind of a situation. You going to be having all of this coming in and you are going to be in this kind of a situation. You going to try to talk to him about "Well what do you think of this?" and he going to be saying to you, "Is very interesting concept, however this is what I having to be working with, and is very intense you know. So please do not be distracting me from this because it is very, very important." Well you going to get cranky. You going to say to him…

The one time I decide to talk about it.

Exactly. You going to say to him, "Look this is very important, very significant. I actually wishing to share with you something of tremendous value, because it will be, make no mistake about it, and all you can be thinking about is yourself."

Mmm.

Well he then going to get cranky because he going to say what he working on is very, very important because once he understands it he can be sharing it with the group of you.

Yes.
You see the perceptions?
Mmm.

Now, you take that into your group situation, you got a lot of random chaos. Have you not? Because everybody going to be thinking what they are doing is the most important aspect of the whole because they are only aware of their own. And they all going to want to be talking together about it, so all of the voices speaking all at the same time. Who is going to be listening?
No one.
And then you got frustration. And then you got the group Dweller.
Yes, the vulnerable point comes out.
Exactly. So, we doing this because you, your partner, your group very good example of what it is we talking about. This is very important information because it is part of the book that this channel is doing. Do you see? It is actually following a theme. You could actually be asking her to let you know about the other pieces.

However, now this is where it gets tricky. You cannot say to your group this is what is going to occur because even if you do they are going to forget about it.
And if you do, they are going to say to you, "Well we are not going to have that kind of a situation. We already done all of that and we are having a good time now." Do you see?
Yes.
So if you say to them that this is really going to be occurring they are going to say to you, "Well do not be so very negative about it." At which point you say, "This John fellow told me to be telling you about it." And they going to say, "Well he being very negative about it and he forgetting we have done

all of this."

Perception again. Do you see? So then what is going to occur, each of you is going to be excessively polite to each other all over again.

Oh no.

Very boring, very, very boring. So what you need to be doing is to be focusing only upon the aspect of the energy that is relevant for you. When you coming to your group situation we would suggest that you ask them to contemplate the formula that you all now working with because you need to adopt a different kind of a formula.

The formula for what?

For your group meditation situation.

Oh, OK. So a different format maybe.

That is so, formula, format. Very well we will remember. Format, very good, very good. You are spending all of this time preparing when you no longer need to do so.

Me?

All of you. You no longer need to do so. In the early stages of the preparation of your energy, the calling in of all of the best guidance you could contemplate, the looking for the messages, was relevant because it was a way of affirming and confirming your own intuitive knowing. Do you see?

Right.

However, it is now not at all necessary. Because what you doing is that you wasting time. Now they are not going to like it when you tell them that. However you can be blaming us, we have no problem about that. You can be using your oil energy for your smudge, you can be using your perfume energy for your smudge, your burning...

Incense?

That is the one. Or you can simply affirm to yourself your energy is clean, and you done it.

Yes.

If you going to have a message, then ask your guidance in meditation for the message.

You mean a channelled message?

Or even your personal message. Each of you now is at the point where you ready to start working individually within the whole energy of the group.

Right.

And by this we speaking of the Australia kind of a energy also. Every member of the total of the group energy is now able to be working individually within it. If you are all going to be doing the same thing, well what are you going to achieve?

So that means that instead of having a set format for a particular meditation we could maybe open together as a group and then do our own thing and then come back and discuss it?

What you do, you have a theme. So whoever, because you been taking it in turns, whoever's turn says to the others, "This is your opening format." - not a formula?

Format is probably better.

Thank you. "This is the opening format. This is the theme I have been told to give to you, do it, now go away to wait. And when you done it all I will call you back, and we will all have a big talking about it."

In the circle?

In the situation itself, that is so. And what you do is you record the information that you getting. Because you will then be beginning to see how is relevant to the whole. In your early stages your perception was you had to do it all together and that is accurate. However now you come to

58

this point you need to be expanding your energy, do you see?

So now what you are doing is that you ready to step into what is a Ray 7 kind of a endeavour.
As the group?
Indeed. Every individual in the group has their own role to play. If every individual does the same thing as everybody else, well you not going to go anywhere. All of you are different. You have your different strengths, your different skills. Now it is time to start putting who you Be into the energy.
Whereas to this point it was more important to learn to connect to each other, to form the energy, now you going to start qualifying that energy by who you Be, do you see? So this is how group endeavour is working.
Right. Because everybody's filter is valid.
That is so. If you are all trying to have the same filter well you wasting your time. Because then you do not need all of you, you only need one of you.

So you all got to have your own filter. You all got to have your own say. You all got to have your own role. Because the group energy is the strength of every individual within it: whereas the perception in your world is if you belonging to a group you all got to become clones of each other.
Yes.

And so eventually you all going to be wearing exactly the same kind of a clothing, having the same kind of a hair, having the same kind of a shoes. What you got? You got nothing, absolutely nothing. It is why your world is in the situation it is in. When we were walking about the place we were not all wearing the same kind of a clothing. We all were different individuals.

Yes, you did not have a beard!

That is so! Why would I be wishing to be having a beard in that lifetime? Very hot, very kind of a difficult situation, do you see? So, now we got to talk about it a little bit deeper.

Perception is very important in your spiritual journey because if you do not have a perception about anything how the dickens are you going to prove it or disprove it?

You will not know where you are either.

Exactly, you see, a belief situation can be a fixed situation. Well you are told this is what you got to believe, so you believe it; until you have a perception about something, which makes you question your belief. So perception is the first stage of the intuition operating within you, because it is coming through the subconscious. Because it is being sneaky coming through the back door, well you already got the perception before you realize you been infiltrated at all. You see?

Mmm. OK.

Then what you do depends upon how open you are being. If your belief system is very rigid and very controlling you going to have such a tremendous fighting with yourself you going to be thinking you losing your plot! If however your belief system has enabled you to feel nurtured within it, then although this perception may be a little bit discombobulating, ultimately you going to see how it proves, enhances, or changes your belief system and in any of those situations you have grown.

Yes.

If you take personally another's disagreement of your perception, in taking personally their disagreement you are closing it down also. Do you see?

This is particularly relevant for my future teaching.

That is so. It is why you getting it, not anybody else, do you see? So we are very, very thankful that you are here so we can be having this conversation.

Now then, you get your perception; you align it to your belief system, one way or the other. You do some manipulating of the energy and now you got a new belief system, based upon a change of perception. That new belief system needs time to become grounded. So, if you go about the place sharing this new belief system with those who you know enjoy the old belief system, well actually you asking for problem.
Yes, OK.

And yet that is exactly what occurs. As soon as you get a kind of a enlightenment you try to go to convert everybody else.....
It is exciting.
Exactly. You are so enthusiastic about it. It is like, "Well I better be going telling as many people as possible so they can be having the same kind of a joy." But there is no discrimination. And in actuality you are not using your perception of these ones to determine who going to be open and who going to be closed.
Or allow you to be open or closed.

That is so. And this is why we say to you please do not be going about the place converting people because then we have to come along behind you and change it all back again. When you trying to do this, in the newness of it, you have not quite fully grounded and understood it, you going to tell people a misperception of how you combined it. And then you going to be quite upset later when you find out what they think you telling them is so different to what you believing. When you have this new expansion and belief spiritually, it is much better to keep quiet about it. You hold the silence because it is in the silence the perception and belief become one.

OK.

And in that silence, you are then able to have deeper recognition of what is only dimly perceived at the beginning of this whole process, conscious beginning of the process.

Waiting for the dust to settle will give you a clearer focus.

Allowing the dust to be settling suddenly becomes very clear. Not only can you see your new belief system, you can see how far it can take you. Because there is no dustiness about the place, and because you can see how far it can take you, you also know there is going to come a point where you got to have a new perception.

OK.

Do you see, because you can see where already there is a potential for a limitation unless you able to work upon another perception to expand again.

So, that means... Am I doing this now?

Indeed you are.

So I should not voice ideas at the moment, I should just wait for them to formulate a bit better?

Because then when you know that they formulated more clearly and you are expressing them, and somebody else says to you, "You have not quite got that right you know," or, "Oh yes I know what you are talking about. I been working with this. However this is my understanding," you are not going to get cranky, feel you not being heard. Do you see?

Instead of that you are going to be saying, "Oh, well that is their perception of it and is valid for them. This is mine and when we put it all together we are going to have a very nice picture of the whole." Does this assist you in the understanding of what has been occurring?

Yes, however...

There is always however, very good.

It does assist me in that it gives me a directive on how I can best allow my own evolution. However, I am still human and it is nice to bounce things off people.

Not a problem bouncing off of other people if you not going to take it personally when they try to change what you putting together.

I get the point. Yes.

So if you are saying something and they taking it and interpreting it in this way, you hold your silence. You can have this kind of a discussion because things will come out of it that will assist you in your own, but you are not taking it personally.

Yes. OK.

Now, if you are able to do this, if you are able to share this with the group situation, then the Dweller of the group energy, which is now about to start having an interplay is not going to be very effective.

Oh, I see. OK.

Because one of the things that it so enjoys the most of all...

The Dweller?

Indeed, are the arguments about perception.

Because that is when we limit each other.

That is so. So of course it is going to be having a party because suddenly you closing the energy down, not opening it all up.

Closing down energy, but opening up also the negative side in that, how dare they do that! Or, you know, dis-validate, or un-validate me.

That is so, when in actual fact by taking it personally you are doing it to yourself. So the Dweller is going to be saying, "Well please to continue. This is a very good situation to be occurring." And so, it is not a coincidence that your partner been meeting this fellow already.

Is that the Dweller for our group?

No, is his Dweller.

Right, OK.

However, his Dweller is the first one of the group who is stepping forward saying, "Well now what are you going to do about me?" And of course your partner saying, "Now I had better think about this." The moment he start to think about it his perception is shifting and changing. He got to keep a detachment.

If he can be looking at this fellow saying, "Well, fine figure of a fellow you be. However I not very interested in coming along your path." Not a problem. If he is sitting saying, "This is a very interesting kind of a situation. I wonder how far this energy is going to take me?" Too late! Totally too late. Do you see? Then he has got to come all the way back again. He is aware of it. He is still playing around with the concept of the whole. However he will understand. His perception of it is going to open. More and more, each of you in your group going to now be dealing with the Dweller on the mental plane.

So be prepared, do you see?

Because the moment you operating in this kind of a manner the Dweller has to be popping up. It is a sign of how far you have all come. Very good! Do not allow your perception of the situation however to discombobulate your knowing of its appropriateness.

OK, so that means that I know that this kind of a situation is right and we are ready for it, so don't try to deny it, just stick with my own perception.

That is so because if you do this you can allow the flow of the energy without becoming entangled in it: whereas if you perceive the situation and say, "Well this is not a good situation to be occurring at this point of time…."

You will block it?

You will go into it. You are not blocking it, you getting caught in it because you are attaching to its appropriateness.

OK, right.

That is very, very, important. So that is all we got to say about perception, do you understand? So we are going to be thanking you for being willing to be of service in this manner. We thank you very much and we leave you.

For I am John.

Notes.

Notes.

Chapter Four
Time

And so, Time to be talking about another aspect of what it is we all doing together.

Time is the aspect of the discussion, do you understand? Do you both understand?

Yes.

We thank you. It is always good to know we have the attention, do you see?

Yes.

We been talking about beliefs, understandings, perceptions, etc., etc. However, we have also at different points of these discussions been talking about the *time* wherein the belief or the understanding or the perception is applicable, do you see?

Because the time is a dimension of your reality, which needs to be understood in the full context of what it is. You use this word often. Many phrases. You got to have time for this. No time. Where has the time been going, do you see? As though time is a physical object, which you can be giving about the place. However, it is a dimension of Being. It has nothing to do with whether you got enough of it or too much of it. It is. It is not an abstract. It is a dimension of your Beingness. Do you see the difference?

Mmm.

Therefore when you are saying that it is time to be doing such and so, that dimension of your Being, which operates in the dimension of time, is knowing that an action is needed to be taken as a part of your Soul Journey.

It is as though you are having a kind of a supervisor, saying to you, "Well, you know, you been having a good time.

However, now you got to stop doing that; you got to start doing this."
It is yours from the perspective only that a part of who you Be inhabits that dimension of reality. Do you see?
Mmm
Because your bodies are operating on all dimensions, or levels, or planes of consciousness, whatever kind of a terminology you wish to be using, you can only claim that aspect of that plane wherein your own energy is in connection to it and you are utilising it.

If you are able to understand it from this perspective, then you are able to recognise that time is, in and of itself, a reality. And now we not speaking about your Earth time. We are speaking about the cycles of time. So when you have your belief system, your perception, your understanding, you are acquiring these according to the time in Earth time, in which you are living, the culture, the race, the belief system that you have chosen to occupy. However, all of these you are choosing as a part of the journey of time, not earth time, cycles of Universal time, that you are following. Because in the final analysis, it is the Universal time, which is governing the period of time in which you are living, do you understand?
Yes.

As a soul, if you choose to learn about slavery, as a consequence of a need to understand subjection, you will be selecting a period of your Earth history (we are presupposing you are going to be born upon your Earth) in which slavery is not only flourishing but it is considered to be acceptable. So you will incarnate during that period. And what is occurring is that you, as a soul, are choosing to learn about slavery during a period when Humanity as a whole is seeking to understand the advantages and the disadvantages of this kind of a consciousness.

So therefore your time is of no moment. The Universal time is governing the Earth for that period of learning. And because you are connected through your 4th dimensional Being to Universal time, you will then gather to yourself a belief or a concept in accordance with that period of Earth time that is learning the Universal aspect of it. Is this simple? Is it too complex?

Can you define 4th dimensional Being?
It is that aspect of your Being that has no physical form. It is a part of your consciousness that inhabits that dimension where Universal cycles of time are the focus of the dimensional energy. Everything is cyclic in that dimension. There is no form as you know form governed by matter. You are moving out of form into energy and its expression or its cycle of Being. So, it is that part of your consciousness that is anchored in that dimension to enable you to interact with it as part of the overall journey of the soul and therefore of the Divine Spark of Being. Does this clarify?
Yes, thank you.
Do you have another question?

Does that principle tie in with the belief that people are living all lives at one time? That there's Universal time but there's all these lives, or past lives, these cycles of Earth time are all running parallel?

That is a belief of consciousness. It has nothing to do with time. It is a belief. When individuals explore time from the perspective of cycles of life and Being they then have to make a decision. Are we going to see everything as

occurring simultaneously or are we going to see everything as occurring consecutively to make it easier to understand? In actual fact, has nothing to do with anything. Do you see? It is simply a construct to enable a belief to be expressed in your world. So to answer your question got nothing to do with it.
Thank you.

I have a question. Did mankind create time because we only have one sun for our planet? Whereas if the planet had 2 suns, there was permanent daylight, time would not matter?

Earth time? Universal time?
No, Earth time.
We are aware of what it is you are asking. Earth time was created for 2 reasons. First of all, you got to go to the beginning of the theory, no point beginning part way through it.

Man did not create Earth time because the Earth only has one sun, because man came to the Earth knowing the Earth only had one sun: to experience a kind of time, which followed the pattern of the Universal knowing. Do you see?
No.
Man did not come to Earth, say, "Oh, the Earth only has one sun. We better create time to be in flow with the seasons". Your Solar System was created with only one sun so that Humanity could learn about cycles of Being and so time was created as a mechanism to understand Universal cycles, brought into a physical Earth dimension to make it simpler to be understood.
When, as a soul in evolution, you are no longer needing to connect to the dimension of time, the 4th dimension, because

now you understand and have mastered it, then you will go to a system where there is more than one sun.

You do not need cycles or seasons because time is no longer something you are learning to master. It is already within you; integrated and fully understood. Do you see?

Yes.

Does this clarify?

Yes.

Then we thank you.

So therefore, if you look at the ages of your Humanity, the few ages that you have any history still remaining, you can see that throughout each age an aspect of consciousness has been learned and time has been applicable to the aspect of consciousness because it has been able then to define the stages of learning within that consciousness, the beginning and the end, do you see?

Right.

Time therefore is extremely significant from the perspective of flowing with the cycle of energy and of no significance when it becomes the master of your destiny. And that is where the people of your world, in their search for spiritual evolution, create their greatest testing. It is why it is so difficult to move beyond the 3rd dimension. Because in order to move beyond it, time must be mastered.

How many times does an individual say, "I truly wish to devote myself to my spiritual journey. Unfortunately, there are not sufficient of my hours to do so because I got to be doing such and so." What they are saying is, "I am still preferring my attachment to the material reality. It is more alive, more real and more vivid. I can come to my spirituality later" because, and here is the irony, they know they have all of the time in the world, this world, to do so; because if

they do not master in this lifetime they can come back again, do it all over again. Do you see?
Mmm.
So it is both a limitation and an initiation. At this period of your Earth history, you are coming to the end of a cycle, Universal cycle, of consciousness. It is a very significant period of your time and of the Universal time because it is an opportunity that is being granted on two levels.

First of all, as you know, it is the opportunity for Humanity to move beyond the emotional into the mental. It is also the opportunity of Humanity to move beyond the concrete; beyond the dominion matter holds over Humanity: to be able to step into the new energy, the new cycle of knowing, which says that the concrete is simply another expression of the Divine. Therefore to place it into its proper time and space, we can move forward, do you see?
Mmm.

So it interesting how such a concept has been limited to what is occurring during the period of your day-to-day situation. Indeed, before you began this particular discussion, a comment was made by this channel, was it not about, "Well, we better be aware of the time". Do you see?

It has become a limitation. She is quite accurate. You have to be aware of the time, simply because if we continue to be talking, talking, talking and you know you got to be going elsewhere, what will occur is both of you will become distracted by your knowing, wonder if we ever going to stop talking, or how you going to be able to interrupt politely, so we not going to be offended and strike you by lightning. Do you see? And so your attention is not upon the topic we are discussing. So the time situation was created initially as a framework in which to operate. And that time frame was the passage of the sun and the moon. It was very simple.

"When the sun is rising we got to be awake. We got to be going about our day-to-day situation. When the sun is going to sleep, well we better go to sleep also, because the moon will then rise. It has an aspect to help us with our spiritual development, whilst we are sleeping." Your world was divided into two time zones, day and night. However, as the world became more complex about what it was creating, "We got to divide this day time situation into certain periods of time because then we can ascertain whether we going to complete the tasks we are setting to ourselves before the ending of the day."

However, then what began to occur was, "Oh, I doing these tasks easily. Obviously I cannot be working hard enough I better be adding some more." Until finally, "I got no time to be doing anything. In fact I still not completed some of the tasks I decided to do the previous day of my time."
And so you are enslaved by time and cannot therefore move beyond your 3rd dimension. There are those who say that time is relevant. Well, of course it is. It is a dimension of Being. Of course it has relevance to consciousness. And so they say that they going to manage this time. Very clever! They going to manage a dimension of Being, by being logical. They cannot. You can manage that aspect of Being by being intuitive and then allowing your mind to utilise that intuition and create a different framework.

However, by being logical about it, you simply going to create another kind of a time prison, do you see? Because you set yourself a time management, it becomes the new prison officer. "Oh well, I supposed to be doing this by this point of my time and I not done it." Therefore you criticise yourselves and you become entrenched in your matter once again. What is needed is for you to forget about time, for a period of your time, and to allow yourself to awaken and to sleep according to the rhythm of your own Being; not your body, your Being. This requires a commitment. What a surprise! It requires you, for a period of 7 days of your time, to disconnect from any of the material, habitual activities, and simply flow with the energy.

So, for example, you know you got to be working for a period of so many hours of your day. You say to yourself, "These are the time frames that have been established. I cannot stop this or everything going to fall apart in the world, if nobody doing their working. However, what I can do is to say that if it is possible in my working situation, then I will attend, I will flow with the work that I do, according to my intuitive understanding of the ebb and the flow of the work itself." rather than, "This is a task which must be performed."

What you will find is that the moment you are flowing with the energy of that aspect of yourself connected to the 4th dimensional Being of time, that you will accomplish more because you forgetting about what must be and allowing what is. And then, of course, in your personal situations, the same thing applies. There are certain requirements that cannot be overlooked and indeed it is necessary not to overlook. For example, you got to be eating. Therefore, there got to be time established for preparation of this food, does there not? If however, you are saying to yourself, "Well, I got to be preparing this food at 5 o' clock of my time every day," 5 o'clock has become a prison. Do you see?

Whereas, if you say, "Well, we gather together. We ask ourselves are we very hungry at the moment? No. Are we going to be waiting until we are, or are we going to say to ourselves that to have a large meal is also a construct of time?" Because your time is divided into your 3 specific meals, is it not? It is simply another division. It becomes another prison. You say to yourself that there must be other ways to explore. "Let's have an adventure and explore how we going to go about it." It does not mean that you got to change what you are doing. We are asking you to become conscious of what you do because of a construct of time and what you do because of a limitation of time. Because once you understand the limitations, you will then be able to see what in your 3rd dimension you are attaching to that prevents you from moving beyond the 4th into the 5th. Do you understand?
Yes, I think so.

That is all it is. When you know and are listening to that aspect of your Being that **is** of the 4th dimension, you will find (this will be quite a surprise!) you are actually more efficient, achieving more, using less energy, having a lot more time for playing about the place than when you allow your 3rd dimensional mind to organise for you. Because you are utilising that aspect of your Being of the 4th dimension, you are in harmony with the cycles. And so, as a consequence, if you need a little bit more time, you can stretch it. If you need a little less, you can condense it because you know you going to find a need for more elsewhere.

Whereas if you rigid and say, "Got to do this, got to do this," there is no room to master time. It is controlling and directing you. And for those who wish to be able to move forward in

their spiritual body, to be able to journey about the place, visit other places to learn, to explore, it is not possible in a safe evolutionary pattern, until you can detach from your earthly time and connect to your Universal time. Then the rhythm of it enables the detaching from the material body to become much easier and away you go. Do you see?
Yes.

It is why time as a topic takes up so much of everybody's time because their guidance is trying to say to them, "Listen to what you saying. Pay attention to your phraseology. Do something about it." What has occurred is that, as your civilisation has moved through the cycles of time, time has suddenly become a god. So you got to worship it. If you do not worship it, well, it might strike you dead.
Because you run out of time.
Exactly the situation! You are running out of time or you having a heart attack because you have no time to breathe. And what occurs is actually quite ironic.

You become so conscious of the lack of time, you decide to create time. Well, that is very good. At least it is the beginning of moving away from the old slavery. So you begin to say, "Let us evaluate how we are spending our time, what we are doing." You having a very good time. Your personality is feeling very happy because you doing something constructive. And indeed you are. You discussing about it, you exploring. All positive. And you create a space so that you got time. Notice the differentiation. You create space. You do not actually create time. You create a space so that you got time. What do you do with it?
Fill it up.
Exactly the situation!

You fill the space up with something that you usually feel that you have to do.

That you previously feel that you have no time for. So you fill up the space then, oh what a surprise! You got no time anymore.

And you fill up the space because to be doing nothing is not allowable. And even if you not doing anything physically, you are filling up the space with your thought. So you are still attached to the material reality because you are thinking, which is your 3rd dimensional, concrete mind.

So, what you going to do? What you going to do is to stop trying to create time but allow yourself to begin to feel time. You can never run out of it because it is Universal and infinite. Because you are an evolving soul, you are always going to have as many lifetimes as you believe you need in order to complete your journey. So therefore you cannot ever run out of time.

If you allow yourself to begin to feel time, you will begin to feel the natural rhythm of your Earth, of the elemental beings of your Earth and of your own elemental creations. You will feel where you are in harmony and where you are not. You will feel where you are at peace and where you are not. And because you allow yourself to **feel** time, you will understand what is needed to move **beyond** time. Do you see?

Yes.

So what you going to do about it? Is it indeed necessary to do anything about it? Can you not simply continue as you all have been continuing?

Well, we can. I feel I've been having some of those experiences already. Now I understand what they are.

You have been touching the edge of it and running away from it because you were able to sense how very big it is. And the bigness of it, if you will, frightened you so you ran away from it.

Yes. That's why I understood. I'm very much attached to something in that, to go there, the Earth, there's this attachment.

Exactly. So what we saying to you is to allow yourself only to feel the time.
Because in feeling time, what you going to discover is that you got a lot more discipline. Without discipline appearing to be authority or power. And you have a problem about power at this point of your time, do you see? There is a confusion you are in the process of resolving. It is another reason why you been running away from what you been touching. That is something for you to ponder.
The bigness of it is also a kind of a power. And if, therefore, you connect to it and fully understand it, well then, you powerful – and you have a fear of that. Because you have not yet fully understood how you wish to share your power.

So if, as individuals, you continue to allow time to be your master, you will allow yourselves always to be controlled, directed by others. Your governments make commitments on your behalf and you say that there is no point saying anything because they not going to listen. They are not listening because you have never used your connection to time to pay attention to what is occurring; and so your governments have quite naturally said, "It really does not matter if we have a discussion with the people about everything because in the final analysis, they got no time to pay attention to us. They too busy in their own worlds. So therefore we might just as well make all the decisions without worrying about these ones." Do you see?

You are so focussed upon the details of your day-to day existence that you are not at all paying attention to the major cycles that are occurring: and the consequences that they have upon your lives. If you were to stop and consider, you are living in a time of the greatest limitation of the individual in the history of your world. There are rules and regulations about every aspect of your life, about everything you can and cannot do. And those rules and regulations have been allowed to be placed there over a period of time because the people themselves have not had sufficient time to pay attention to what is occurring and to voice their approval or objections.

You do not live in a world of freedom. And you cannot live in a world of freedom until you master time. Anything else is simply the banging of your head upon your wall and then in your frustration, what you do is you seek for an outlet and then you focus your frustration or discontent, whatever terminology you care to be using, upon someone or something else simply because you are not being in time with yourself. Now when you are in time with yourself, completely different kettle of your fish. When you are in time with yourself, your natural vitality flows freely. Your immune system is strong, so therefore there are no disease energies interpenetrating your physical matter because your consciousness is vibrating at the 4th dimension not the 3rd where disease manifests. So, if you wish to avoid disease, you need to be in tune with time.

As a consequence, because you are stronger in your vitality, your system is stronger, you are able to accomplish more.

Because your thinking is clearer, your emotional energy is flowing, you are not creating this kind of a stress, tension about what you not doing, could, should or ought to be doing. You are not in that consciousness. You are at peace and in flow. We are not saying you got to live without time at all. We are saying that time is very important. Universal time, 4th dimensional flow of energy flowing through your 3rd dimensional Being and enabling you to manipulate time, to master time, to bend it to what it is you are seeking to achieve. That is when you are effective fully and completely in your world. Do you have any question about it?

It seems like the saying that if it feels good, do it. From a time point of view you're going with your intuition and feeling rather than the logic, which asks if I've got time to do it.
That is so.
So if you follow that through, as you've just said, because you're going with the feelings, the intuition, the more you allow that to happen the better, quicker, your intuition will develop and then you'll move through 4th and 5th dimensions.
That is so.

The one aspect you got to be careful about is that you use the feeling of time as a reason to avoid responsibility in the 3rd dimension. "Oh, well, I cannot be preparing this whatever it is that you are asking me to do because, you know, I'm feeling time at the moment. And in my feeling of time, that is not part of my reality." It's never going to work because you going to have chaos, do you see? It is saying, "I am feeling the rhythm of time. This is something I am being asked to do." (We talking about a working situation). You are being asked to do a particular task. What you do is you feel the energy of time as it flows through you in relationship to the task and perform it in the timeless manner of the

Universal, rather than the slavery of time of the earthly.

Could you give an example?

Just supposing you been asked to be driving from A to B. Is not a very difficult journey, perhaps it's going to take you half hour of your time. However, it is part of something you are being asked to do. If you say to yourself, "Well, it's going to take me half hour of my time. Then I got to do such and so and this and so. I can be back at my place of employment at such a time." Your concrete mind has already analysed the situation and determined how long you going to be and when you going to be back. You have set a limit upon your Being. If you are feeling the time through the cycle of time, you may say to your employer or whoever, "This journey normally takes approximately 30 minutes of my time. However, today I am going to see how the energy is flowing so that I can see how much can be accomplished before my return." Not from how much you got to do but as an observation, not an attachment.
Your employer says to you, "Do you think you going to be returning within a couple of hours of our time?" "Most certainly, it can be done. However, not quite certain specifically when." Because at this point you do not know. You still playing with time. Do you understand?

Yes. It just raises another question.

Let us complete this first. So, you get into your vehicle and you attune yourself to that dimension of time that is Universal. You begin to breathe with the rhythm of that Universal energy. You do not go into a meditative situation. You simply breathe 2 or 3 times, allow yourself to relax. You tell yourself that you not going to think about what you going to do when you get there, you simply going to focus upon the journey and enjoy what you are observing. You are then allowing the energy to flow through you and you find you getting there quicker. You doing what you got to do. Each task in its time of Universal time. And then you returning.

If you practise this, you will find that one day you going to be asked to make this journey, your employer going to say to you, "Well, you know, you got to go here, do such and so. How long do you think you going to be missing?" You are intuitively going to know exactly when you are going to return because now you are accustomed to that vibration and you not attached to whether you going to get caught, whether somebody going to be talking, talking, talking, you cannot get away. You just going to know you are non-attached to the 3rd dimension and you just going to move through it. You got to practise it, do you see?

In that scenario that's very understandable. What about when other people put time restrictions on you? For example, you know and your employer knows that it's going to take you 30 minutes to do this task but your intuitive Being wants to be 2 hours, would like to be as long as it feels it's good but your employer says no that you have to do this and come back. You have to be back here by a certain time, quicker than you would desire to be out. Another example, you are going to go to the corner store for a bottle of milk. You and your partner know it's 10 minutes but you may be desirous of going for a ride and sit on the beach for half an hour, thus being out for perhaps an hour. Your partner has a problem with that because it should only take 10 minutes and why didn't you come straight back?

You are confusing the situation. First of all, you are using in your second example a dishonesty. Because if you have spoken to your partner that you going to collect some milk and yet you have the intent to be riding about the place, then you are not being honest. Of course your partner is going to have a problem about it. However, to return to the initial example, once you practise the use of being in tune with time, of the 4th dimension, as we were saying earlier, then you can condense time. You may feel that is going to take you about 2 hours to do this task, in order for you to have the benefit of it. So what you do in your consciousness is step out of Earth time. For you it is as though you are 2 of these hours but in your Earth time it is only 30 of your minutes. That is where you move beyond it. In the 2nd example, you are saying to someone, "I going to do this." And then you choose not to do it because you felt in tune with the time. That is what we were saying earlier. Do not use it as an excuse because that is what it is.

When you are in tune with time, does not mean that you discard your responsibilities. It does not mean that you use it as an excuse to simply please yourself at the expense of those about you. If you wish to do nothing, if you wish to be journeying, if you wish to be daydreaming, then it is necessary to say, "This is what I am choosing to do at this point of my time. Do you have a problem about it?" And if your partner says to you no then very good. If your partner says, "I have a problem because these are things that need to be attended to." Then you discuss together how you going to do so. Do not say, "Well, you got to do them because I being in tune with time." Else you are becoming a persecutor. You say that when you done with being in tune with time, you can share what needs to be done.

The whole purpose, however, is not to stop doing things. It

is to find the rhythm, the true rhythm, of the action you are doing because as you align yourself to it, your Earthly time becomes non-existent. You complete more speedily. You do not take longer. Because you are in tune with the activity you are performing, you complete it more speedily. And then, what a surprise! You got more time. Do you see? Does this clarify for you?

Yes.

It is the danger that is inherent within each individual, to see such a concept and to say, "Oh very good. Now it gives me an excuse to do even less."That is not the situation. You look at the task, the energy of the task, and then you feel the energy of that timelessness of the 4th dimension, which is true time. You align the two together and you flow with it. Suddenly everything completed and you not even aware of what you doing. It is effortless. And because everything becomes effortless, you can leave your body, go all over the place because you not attached to it or its outcome. Do you see?

Do you have any questions? Or have we put you out of your time?

No, I understand it. It makes sense to me. I've had some experiences of that.

So, therefore, both of you going to be completing lots of things, sometimes before you think you even started!

Yes. I've experienced that too.

That is the reality of the situation. That is what is being 4th dimensional.

That is good clarity. I think that's been a bit of confusion about 4th dimensional too. It's more of a concept I'd like to understand more clearly and that has.

Basically, that is it. The confusion is because lot of your people have access to this 4th dimensional aspect and in accessing it believe that it then means they simply got to do nothing of a Earth time. They got to detach from the Earth time, with responsibility also. Well, you know, that is confusion.

What you are doing is you bringing the 4th dimensional energy into the 3^{rd,} so that you can be moving through your 3rd dimension, in rhythm that enables your Soul to evolve beyond it. You do not use it to get out of your 3rd dimension, so you having a good time in the 4th and the 5th, and suddenly we have to be throwing you back to the 3rd because you do not wish to be there. Do you see?

One is an avoidance, a disclaiming of responsibility: the other is an integrating of the energy of who you Be at the 3rd and who you Be at the 4th. It is climbing the ladder. So, when we been talking in the past about the cycles and how the beliefs, the attitudes, judgments of particular eras of time have had an impact upon the spiritual evolution, now you can understand why. Because in each of these cycles, there reaches a point where time must be mastered: and rather than being mastered, the energy begins all over again.

Someone suddenly says, "Oh, I got a good idea you know about this time." Everybody says, "Oh, that is a very good idea we going to do it." And in time you find they all doing exactly what they were doing previously. They just got a different label for it. This point of your Earth history is another major opportunity to move beyond Earth time: to understand exactly what the Universal energy of the time is and what it requires. Not to simply feel it and say, "Oh well." To feel it and then to say, "I understand what is this energy. How therefore can I put it into action? Where can I incorporate this Universal energy in my day-to day situation?" That is how you expand the consciousness of your planet.

So, each time you come to this kind of a point in time, there is an opportunity for more enlightenment, for the Light to flourish. Often what happens is that the opportunity is misunderstood and you get darkness, not Light, which is exactly what is occurring at this point of your time. However, the Light will shine through the darkness, as the glimmers of understanding become greater. That too is part of the cycle of time. So, is there anything you wish to ask about? Or can we come to a close of your time?
No, I have no questions.
I don't have a question, in the sense that I understand it. I'm trying to think of a question because it's going in the book.

Do not try. Because you know there going to come a time when everything that been done to this point of your time, going to coalesce within you and then you going to ask, both of you, a few questions.
Oh, and then it will be the next part. It's the process.
Do you see?
Yes, I do.
You trying to pre-empt time. Well, you never going to pre-empt it.
No, they keep telling me.
You got to flow with it.
That's right.

There is one thing we will say to you, however, nothing to do with the book but to do with you. You are quite accurate in your understanding that you not got to think about it. However, you do need to feel the timeliness of it. Do you

understand?
Timeliness. Not quite.
Part of you is feeling that you know it is something that is important. It is bringing up within you concepts to consider, emotions to experience. Do you notice this phraseology? Concepts to consider, emotions to experience. You do not have to rationalise or justify them. Just allow them. And so you are aware that it is a process.

Part of your confusion lies in the fact that you are not aware of why this process is timely for you, at this point of your time. And so as a consequence there is a part of you creating a kind of a subconscious judgment, which makes for you an uncomfortable emotion, which then creates a kind of a sense of distance around you. Do you understand? You are not creating it. The subconscious judgment and the emotion attached to it are creating a kind of a distance around you, which then creates for you a need to continue to experience, without fully recognising that it is exactly appropriate in time for what you are undergoing. Do you understand?

Yes, I think so. I understand that it's timely; the distance, I thought, was a part of it.

Not at all. When you are in time, you do not detach from what is occurring around you. You detach from the belief of how long it has got to take. Do you see the difference?

Can I give an example and then you come through there? Please to do so. Actually this may go into the book, you know. We may just have to do this. However, please give to us your example.

OK because I felt I was set up with Spirit. I felt all of a sudden that I had to go in and write, into the meditation room. As I let it flow, I felt, I actually took off my watch too, I was writing for ages. I was in this space. There was no time. When I came out, I'd only been in there for 20 minutes and that really surprised me. So could you come through with that?

No.
OK.
That is a good example of how, when you flow with the time, the Universal time of the task, you can condense time. You feel as though you been there forever. Suddenly you find hardly any time at all. So that is a good example of the earlier part of that which we talking.

However, because you know you are going through a process, and you know it's taking you somewhere, and part of you has touched it and it feels very big to you. So well, "I do not want to touch it too well because I then might see it. Then what the dickens I going to do about it?" That is a natural part of the process do you see? However, you are allowing the rhythm of the energy to flow but a part of you is standing in judgment of yourself about what you are thinking and feeling and observing.
OK. Yes.

And so, because you are standing in judgment about it, there is an emotion you feel as a consequence. Because of these two, what you have done (or what these two have done, because you consciously have not), is begun to weave a distance around you to insulate you because even though you going to observe, you not going to feel judgment or emotion as continuously. What you have done is you have tried to detach from the people and the situation, rather than detaching from the time it is taking on that journey.

There is nothing wrong in observing and having your thoughts and feelings. They will move through you irrespective of anything you choose to do because of who you Be, is who all of you Be. You are always going to have a thought and a feeling about what you doing, what you thinking, what other people thinking. As a consequence, it is part of the rhythm of the timeliness of the activity. If you were not having these thoughts and feelings you could not be going through a process. Because a process involves a time.

So at the beginning of the process, often there is a kind of a denial. Then as you move through it you begin to get a glimmer of an understanding. Then you begin to have thoughts and emotions. Then you begin to judge the thoughts and the emotions. Then it becomes a confusion. Then finally you find a kind of a peace. Then you have the answer. You are at the part of the process where part of you is judging what you are experiencing in your observations. So therefore you are attaching to that which gives you a sense of discomfort because you have judged it. Whereas if you observe it and when you have a feeling about it say to yourself, "That feeling is very interesting. There is something in there for me to explore when the time is appropriate." You are seeing the feeling and because of the judgment it has become an attachment, which more and more kind of insulates you. So even though you are connecting to people, you are not connecting to people and places as deeply as you used to do. Do you see?

It does not mean you are less caring. It does not mean you are less loving for it is always who you Be. It is that there is a kind of a shield being woven around you. And a part of you has come to feel that it is necessary as a part of the process for your understanding. However, if you allow yourself to attune to the time and the rhythm of the process you are undergoing, to recognise that the emotions that you feel when you have a recognition are part of the process of helping you to understand yourself in greater detail as well as others, which you do know, then you will dispense with the shield because you will see that it is insulating you against the process: therefore against time.

You have to move through what you are moving through. It is part of your journey and a very important part of your journey. However, if you insulate yourself, if you detach then when you have completed the process, you will find that the shield has become so fixed in place that you cannot take it away. And you will then feel a sense of loss about yourself. Not about what you do, not about your relationships with others. You will feel it as though you have lost something important to you. As indeed you will have. Do you understand?

Bits and pieces. However, I'm going to let that work with the process that's been given.

Work with the timeliness. Because it is all in perfect time and space. However, that is another topic for another day. At this point it is very timely. What we are saying to you, do not allow the timeliness of the process to become another prison. When you come out of it, well you better have your bicycle in very good order. You going to be speeding along the place. And so, is there anything further?
No, I think that was very good for the book though.
We quite agree. That is so. Perhaps we got to ask your permission to use this in the book after all.

Yes, too easy.

Well then, suppose we better say to you we run out of time. How about that? What do you think?

It's perfect Universal time.

The rhythm of the energy has been expressed. Now it is for you to practise with it, do you see? Play about with it and see what occurs. We thank you for being willing to be part of this monologue, because it's not truly a dialogue, you both too quiet about it.

And we look forward to another discussion during this week of your time. So we thank you. Go with our Blessing and our Love until we meet again.

For I am John.

Notes.

Notes

Chapter Five
Space

And we bid you welcome. It is very good to be able to continue with the topics of our discussion, to be able to amplify upon that which has already been given and to extend therefore the frame of reference of what it is we are seeking to share with you. What is being given through the topics of discussion of this volume is a means of moving through the levels of initiation: levels of initiation, which enable mastery to be achieved in your world.

Throughout each of these discussions it has been our purpose to provide a foundation of understanding upon which personal experience can be gathered and built to form the individual's frame of reference for the soul evolution. Do you understand?

I think I do.

As a consequence, we been discussing about your physical, your emotional, your mental in the context of your Earth plane experience and of the cycles of Universal Time. And so, now we come to Space, do you see?

In order to be able to have a clear understanding, it not only necessary to be able to understand time and its mechanism, but it is also necessary to understand Space. And we not speaking about Space from the context of what you able to observe through your physical vision and the use of telescopic instruments. The physical Universes are simply aspects of Space, which are able to be seen and to be understood through the physical phenomena of your body. We are speaking of Space as it exists; not as a physical area that is defined through a form, a matter. Do you understand?

I think so.

Space itself is represented by your Universes. In the same manner that your Earth time became a vehicle, a means of understanding and interpreting Universal time, so your Space, and exploration of it, is simply another vehicle for understanding Universal Space or consciousness. Do you see? Does this clarify for you?
Yes, thank you.

Then we are very happy about it. So, Space itself is that which is understood, in your world, by planes of consciousness, dimensions of Being, whatever terminology you wish to be using. When you talking about Space you talking about Being. Therefore in order to understand Being, it is an advantage to explore Space. And just as in your spiritual evolution you are asked to understand the dimensions of your Being, so in the understanding of your purpose, in the understanding of your growth, do you need to explore Space within and around you. It is being done at a worldly level through your scientific community and its exploration of space, its understanding of planetary energies, how creation is occurring and how things fall into decay. Only now are your scientists beginning to recognise that at the end of the life of a Being in this space, and by Being we are talking about a planetary body or even a system, as they are exploring they are seeing that at the ending of the lives of these, matter is dispersed and then gradually it is reformed. And suddenly you got the beginning of another planetary body or Being.

Therefore in your understanding of Space, the macrocosm, you are actually – if you willing to view it in such a manner – being given a perfect example of reincarnation in action that you can then utilise to understand what occurs for your own progress. Do you see?

Yes.

Obviously the spirit, the soul occupies a physical body for a period of time. When the learning is completed the body decays, falls apart because the spirit is leaving. And then at the appropriate time, after it has all returned to matter and the soul chooses to reincarnate again, matter is gathered around the nucleus of the energy of the soul and away you go again.

However, Space in and of itself is a difficult topic to comprehend because the very vastness of its Being creates an impossible kind of a topic of study for your average individual. Is this not so?

Yes. I think it's like we're trying to comprehend an infinite object with a finite mind.

That is so. And you know, when you are seeking to evolve spiritually, being told, "Well you know, if you do not complete in one lifetime, you can return and complete again," creates the same kind of difficulty of comprehension. Because you are in a finite body with a finite mind, the **theory** of reincarnation is able to be grasped. However, the understanding of it creates difficulty, do you see?

Yes.

What occurs is that the individual becomes fascinated by what are the possibilities and can also be seduced by who they have been in previous incarnations. Have they been famous? Have they achieved anything of worldly renown or significance? Are they living a particular life as a source of punishment? What is occurring is that the finite mind is trying to grasp an infinite concept by focusing upon detail.

When you are seeking to understand yourself as a Being, detail can be misleading. Until and unless you can grasp that the infinite possibilities of all you are, all you can be, all you have been are housed within who you being now, all else is simply a kind of a diversion of your mind to enable you to try to grasp some kind of understanding. And so you are simply circling around the whole situation, do you see?

So, how to make it simple?
Well, you know, the answer most truly is that you cannot.
It is a complex topic. What can only be achieved is to create a kind of a situation wherein the individual begins to play with the idea from the concept of 'what if.' And to do this, guidance is offered to enable each soul to begin to try to understand the whole by understanding the part. The part that is who that individual be.

For example, you know that you have had a birth; that you have had parents who have been there for you to help you to grow; to move through cycles of your time in accordance with the life purpose and energy. You reach a certain point of your time and at that point you know, if you have this kind of a belief, that you going to leave your body: that you will then perform a kind of a review of the life previously just lived. And then you going to determine what you got to complete, what you did not even begin to work upon, what you totally achieved before you can then decide whether you going to take another body and what you going to do with it when you got it.

That is simple because not only do you have evidence of your own physical life, you have those individuals such as this channel who are able to be mediums for those who are departed to return to give messages of comfort, of assistance, of guidance. So, there is a knowing that consciousness continues even though the proof is lacking until it is the individual's turn to make that journey. Is this not so?

Yes.

In order therefore to allow yourself to expand your consciousness, you must go within your own sense of Being to truly explore Space because Space simply is Spirit. If you study your physical universes, then you can become totally engrossed in the creation of matter. If you think about it, even the idea of visiting another of your planets of your Solar System is becoming more conceivable through time. And yet it is still inconceivable because there no true idea of how you going to get there and what you truly going to experience when you do. And so, in order to understand Space, the focus becomes entrapped by the kind of a distraction of studying how you can explore it in a physical body.

In order to truly understand it, you can only explore it within your **own** physical body. And this is where your meditative situation, your creative visualisation kind of an energy, your contemplation are tools to enable such an exploration to be occurring. By using these tools to go within your own Being, you step into Space. Is this clear?

And the Space is described in many ways, dependent upon the method being utilised, dependent upon the consciousness of the individual. When you withdraw your physical attention and focus from the external, and begin to allow yourself to go within, you feel an expansion of your Being, do you not?

You do.

That is because you are withdrawing your consciousness from the limitation of your physical form. You are no longer utilising physical senses. You are no longer limited by the extent and the ability of those senses. The moment you begin to focus within, your whole consciousness becomes open to you. You are not growing. You are simply becoming aware of how much more of you there is than you are aware of when in your physical form and fully conscious in your day-to-day situation.

However, simply going within and feeling this expansion of consciousness does not give to you any further depth or detail about Space. It simply proves to you that when you are in such a situation you become more aware of your Space, do you see?
Yes.

In order therefore to understand Space itself, it is important to be aware of what is occurring to you at a physical level when you go within. By becoming aware of what is occurring to you at a physical level, you are then gradually being able to discard the sense of limitation, which attaches your soul to the physical form, and once you are aware of it, as with Time and being in tune with it, you can move beyond it. There are many ways of doing this, you know. For example, some of the ancients would spin. In spinning around and around they were able to lift their consciousness to a kind of an ecstasy. At that point of ecstasy or joy, they stepped out of their physical body, the body would fall to the ground and they would thus be able to move at will wherever they wished to be going; to explore any dimension of being, dependent upon the purpose for doing so.

So, for example, what is called a shaman would be leaving the body in order either to be learning more about Universal Law governing matter and the physical or to have a understanding of what is occurring within a specific situation by studying the Akashic records and returning with the knowledge thus to be shared with those about. The intent therefore is of prime importance when seeking to explore Space because your intent at the point of doing so will determine where you find yourself once you got out of your physical form.

Why would you wish to do so? What is the purpose? You are in a physical body. Why would you wish to explore Space, to step out of it, to be going about the place and then to be returning? Would this not simply be reinforcing how very limited in the physical you are? Well, you know, for your world to evolve and grow, individuals are always leaving their physical bodies for one purpose or another and then bringing back to the physical with them what it is they can access that enables your civilisation to move further along the path of evolution. It is not a kind of a exercise that we would recommend simply for the sake of curiosity. Because as in any kind of a learning situation, if you only going for curiosity into the situation, you are not necessarily going to be disciplined, you not necessarily going to be aware of the disturbances that you could encounter.
Therefore you could find yourself in serious kind of difficulty.

In the journey of the soul's evolution, however, there comes a point where the individual is required to be able to demonstrate the ability to step out of the body, at will, according to the circumstances, to show mastery of the physical form finally. And then to step back into it because the individual still has to continue to be sharing with those about him what has been achieved, what is possible.
All of the Master Teachers of your time have been able to leave their physical form at will. Not because they wished to be having a holiday, but because in order to be leaving

the body, they have been able to be showing others how to do so and thus expanding, widening, the link between Spirit and the Earth for information to be shared with your Earth. It is the only true purpose for this kind of a work. Those who seek to be travelling about the place in their spiritual body, their etheric energy, for no other purpose than to be simply curious about situations, are not contributing to your world as a whole and its evolution. They may contribute knowledge. They may misunderstand what it is they have seen. If there is no spiritual discipline in the journeying itself, then what is being shared has no true understanding to support it. And so many can be led astray.

Whereas, if there is an intent and a purpose, the exploration of the Space, of the Spirit, is a marvellous aid to enlightenment. Now, in order to understand this Space more easily, we will use the example of your physical body.
When you incarnate, and as you grow...we not going to talk about the formation of the body in the womb, that is easily to be researched and understood, so many amounts of information about it. What is of significance about it, however, is that the brain within you could be deemed kind of a symbol of your Central Sun because it the place of your enlightenment. Do you see? And from the centres of your head you are making your connection to the Universe. However, your brain itself also extends into the physical body so it is housed in your head, goes down through the spine, and is therefore able to have direct influence and bearing upon everything that you are doing at every point of your time. Whether you be awake or asleep, your brain is always functioning.

Your hands may not know what is the brain. They may simply know that impulses of energy are able to control and direct them. And the cells within your fingers may not know anything about the rest of your body in full consciousness. However, those cells are impacted as a consequence of the messages being transmitted by the brain. Is this not so?

Yes.

So therefore, in your meditative situation, if you were to take your focus into a particular cell of your body that cell would have a kind of a hologram of the whole but it would appear to be quite nebulous. Do you see?

I think that might need clarification.

We will do so.

You go into the cell. In that cell there is a consciousness that is a part of a greater whole. However, its purpose is quite clearly defined so it's going about its business doing everything it's supposed to be doing, whilst still having a kind of a understanding that it is part of a greater whole. Therefore, as you become one with that cell, you will know what you doing in your day-to-day situation, as it were, and you are aware of a greater whole but because the cell of the hand, of the finger, is not at the centre of the brain it does not know all there is to know. It simply has an awareness behind everything it is doing. Does this clarify?

Yes. Thank you.

Therefore it is the same kind of a situation as the individual and Space. The cell occupies a physical space. However, within it it contains all the information about everything else in smaller or greater degree according to its function. It cannot therefore be speaking to you about All That Is. It can be speaking to you about its awareness that there is more and a subtle kind of an idea about what the more might be. All it can truly share with you is what its full purpose is because that is known.

You, as a individual, are like that cell. You are aware of who you Be as the individual: as the cell is aware of who it be according to its role. You are aware that you have to be performing certain functions as a result of incarnating; that there is a purpose greater than your own with which you are trying to align yourself. Yet you are not totally certain what it may be whilst striving towards that understanding of the greater whole.

It is the same in your Space, your Universal kind of an energy. If you look at your planetary systems, each system has its component parts. So, you have a Solar System with a sun. We will presuppose there is only one to avoid confusion. The planets are circulating about the Sun, just as the cells in the blood circulate about the body. Each cell is aware of its purpose and function and of the path it must take in its moving through the body itself, just as your planets are aware of the path of their orbit, of their function as they are moving around the Sun.

Now in your Universal energy you got what are called Solar winds. Well, they not simply Solar winds. You got a Solar wind for your Solar System. However, there are winds that are Universal currents of energy that are moving about the place all of the time. These winds have seeds of life within them. So wherever they blow they are bringing new life to what is in existence. They are bringing the seeds of life to what is beginning to come to form. As these winds blow, so each planet, each body floating about in space at some point or another feels the energy of this wind as it is blowing about.

As that energy is felt by that planet, some of the seed of that energy attaches to the planetary body. As a

102

consequence, the seeding of the energy of that wind falls to the planetary body itself, in this case your Earth, and every living organism upon the Earth is seeded by that system.

So, you walking about the place. You may not be aware that the Solar wind blowing about the Earth because it is so subtle. And yet, even though it's so subtle, you, as a physical organism, are reacting or responding to it all of the time. It is the same with the cell within your body. According to the kind of energy that you putting into your body, so the cell of your body going to be influenced. And so, either that cell is going to be enhanced, happy, dancing about on its journey or gradually it's going to wither. It will either malfunction, create a kind of a disease because it becomes distorted, or it simply going to feel the life energy is not being received and it will deplete and die.

Well, of course you know, every aspect of who you be is living and dying all of the time. You are aware of this.

Yes.

So you are continually being renewed and reborn just as your planet is continually being seeded by the energy of these winds. These winds are part of what is called Space. These winds are important because they moving energy about all of the time. In terms of your Earth time, they are oxygenating your Universes. It is not exactly oxygenating. However, it is a simple kind of a analogy.

So therefore by taking your consciousness within your Being, you can actually move into the cell and then beyond the cell into Space. Into the exploration of the vastness of your reality that is encapsulated in the cell that is constantly being fed, not simply by what it is you are doing but by what the Universe is doing in its effect upon your planet. It is a true cycle of life, do you see? Nothing is forgotten. Nothing is omitted. Everything is connected.

If your intent is to explore Space so that your understanding can be enhanced and your service to your world improved, and that intent is based upon the will to achieve good in your world, then you can visit what are called your Akashic records. You can literally by going deep within, through the cells of your body, into your connection to Space, view all that has ever been, is or will be. And just as we have used the analogy of the brain and its energy flowing into the torso of the body to stimulate and activate the physical form, so we will use the same analogy to describe what occurs when you leave the space of consciousness of being a human being.

When the brain ceases to function energy is withdrawn from the physical form. Indeed, as the brain begins to die the function is gradually withdrawn little by little into itself, therefore closing down the systems that it has been using. As it withdraws into the head, and the energy no longer transmitted down through the spinal column, the physical body begins literally to die. Because of course when no energy going to the heart, the heart not pumping any blood, the brain is not being enlivened by the blood and so it is a mutual kind of a system, do you see?
Yes.
What occurs then is that the link between the brain and the body is broken.

Well you know, is the same with your physical body and your soul. When your soul begins to withdraw from your physical body because the consciousness of occupying that body has been achieved, it gradually steps out of the body. Disconnection to the physical is through what is called your

Silver Cord.

Well, your Silver Cord is just like your spinal cord. As it withdraws, you can be moving about all over the place and whilst ever your Silver Cord attached to your physical body you going to get back into it. When you finished with it however, you step out of your physical body knowing that you no intentions of returning and that by staying away from the physical body, gradually the Cord going to perish and you going to be free of it. At that point your physical body then can be decaying and returning to matter. And if you choose to be burning it upon your funeral pyre it make no matter because it still going to return to matter, do you see?

Indeed, yes.

You are leaving your physical body behind because you no longer have a need for it. That is because you are changing your consciousness and your physical body is representative of what you are leaving behind because you mastered it. You, as an essence of Being, occupy a different dimension of your Being and so you could say you return to Space, because you not in form.

Well, you know, the same situation occurs with your planetary bodies. You have these black holes in your Space. Your scientists see these as very dangerous kinds of things. It is simply another analogy. If you look at it, your planets disappear into these black holes. Everybody thinks they gone, that is the end of the situation. They simply moving into another dimension of Being. They going to reappear at another time, in another form, as part of the evolutionary growth of the Universe itself. Is this clear?

Mmm, very.

Do you have any questions about what we been talking about?

One thing comes to mind. Just to back track a bit in the conversation, you were saying that every cell in the body knows its purpose and has a consciousness. You mentioned the blood and that every cell in the blood has a consciousness and knows its purpose. What is the case with someone who gives blood or even receives blood? Someone that gives blood, then the blood that is given, the cells within that blood have a consciousness as part of that body. Then they are removed from that body before the cell dies or has lost its consciousness.

Blood's consciousness is life giving. Therefore when you are giving your blood to another, the blood cell itself in its purpose is conscious only of being life-giving.
Oh, OK. All right.

However, the blood contains your vibration. We use you as a example. The blood contains your vibration. So you have given some of your blood in order to be of service to others who may be having a need of it. The intent therefore when you go to be giving your blood is that you are giving it with love for whatever may be needed by whoever may need it. Is this not so?
Yes.
The very fact that your intent is to do so, that you are not limiting or conditioning it, means that that blood is then imbued with Universal consciousness. It ceases to have your consciousness. It becomes Universal because you are saying that you no longer require this. You are offering it to whoever may have a need. You are being unconditional. The moment therefore that blood is leaving your body it ceases to carry the total consciousness of who you be and begins to take on a kind of a neutral consciousness, which is an actual fact the Universal consciousness of Love.

And so, when it is given to another individual, it enters into that individual's system as Love, as Life. Where there is a rejection of the blood by the individual, it is because the individual is rejecting life. The organs are a different kettle of your fish.

Your blood, however, has a very clear understanding. If when you giving your blood, your intent is that you giving this blood and is only to be used by such and so individuals and you make it clear "I'm only giving this blood because of this situation", that blood is conditional. It cannot take upon itself a Universal energy of life. It can only manifest a conditional energy of life and so when it is given to another individual, if that individual accepts it, it is because that individual is equally as conditional as are you. Do you see?

Yes.

If the individual rejects it, either that individual is unconditional or, and this is where is a very tricky kind of a situation, the blood has been given to an individual whom you have not agreed to donate it to. Do you see? Because the blood knows what is going to be given for. So, for example, if you are – we use your modern history – if you are an Arab and you going to give blood and you only going to give blood for those who are Arabian; and suddenly that blood given to somebody who is not Arabian, could be American, for example, well, you know, that blood is not going to work upon that American.

More is going to be needed to be given. It will prove to be insufficient because the condition upon which it was given was not met. Do you see?

Yes.

It poses quite a different light upon things, does it not?

It certainly does.

If you are conditional in your giving of this energy, then you going to have to account to yourself for these conditions at some point of your time. However, that is a different kind of a discussion altogether.
Does this answer your question?
Yes. Thank you.
You are very welcome. Do you have another question about it?

No, not a question. I have a comment that the black hole is very enlightening. I won't say interesting. As you say, what happens to the planet when it explodes or implodes and then it goes through, becomes or goes into a black hole, it is actually the death of that planet. The passage of the black hole is actually equivalent to our reincarnation.

That is so. And just to give you something more to be pondering, you have around your planet holes appearing in your atmosphere, do you not?
Indeed.
They open and then they close, appear somewhere else. There been lot of discussion and concern because they seem to be very, very damaging. What is occurring is when they are opening energy is coming into the Earth that could not enter while they were closed. Now your scientists are saying this is very detrimental to your planet.
Yes.

Well, you know, it has been occurring for millennia. At the time when there is a change of consciousness, a major change of a life cycle, this kind of a situation, then you will have these holes opening. What occurs, energy comes into the planet, for its growth, development; and there will be energies, which are released from the planet, which are no longer required because the energy of the whole is changing. These energies therefore must be discarded. So you could say that these holes are a kind of a black hole in miniature. Do you see?

Mmm, yes.

And, you know, when you leaving your physical body, when your Earthly life is over, you going through a tunnel, are you not?

Yes.

Well, that is another black hole in miniature. Very clever is it not?

It's all a bit tricky.

It is extremely so because everything that you are seeing on a major scale is occurring on a minute scale. Nothing is unconnected.

Mmm. It's true that we are the microcosm and outside is the macrocosm.

That is so.

Outside being Space.

Well, you know, we going to give you another little analogy. Your scientists are spending lot of their money and their energy upon exploring your Space, trying to explore your deep Space; trying to make connection to any other intelligences which might be inhabiting this area etc., etc. are they not?

They are.

And yet you got deep Space on your planet Earth that is only now beginning to be explored. And there are creatures within this deep Space, within the Earth, that have far more intelligence than your human kind considers to be possible. And no attempt is being made to make connection to these intelligences, for learning and sharing of information. When this kind of work does occur it's going to bring about a kind of a revolution in thinking, in consciousness, upon your planet. Then you will discover that the greatest secrets have been in your grasp all of the time. You just never bothered to look. Too busy exploring externally to be bothered to delve into the wonders that lie within.

And that is exactly the same with your human beings; too busy exploring externally, hoping to find the answers to their spirituality, when all they got to do is explore the deep Space within their Being. There lie all of the answers they are seeking.

Mm, yes. Absolutely.

Can you think of any kind of a question you wish to be asking? Or do you feel this is quite sufficient for this time?

I can't think of anything in relation to the topics we've just discussed. It all makes sense to me and in hearing it, it's what I basically believed anyway.

That is fortunate.

Yes, I don't have any sort of...it's difficult to think of a question when I can understand and accept what you are saying.

Then perhaps we can ask you what do you feel with how we have expressed? Is it in simple enough terms – and we not being rude about it – simple enough terms that it could be easily understood by others?

I believe so but it's also as you.... when I have asked you this question before about explanations. And I agree with you. Basically your comment was that there will always be people who will find it too easy, too simplistic an explanation. And there will be others that just don't comprehend it.

That is so.
I think it's OK.
Then that is good.
I can't say it needs to be clearer or it's too simple.
Then we will leave it exactly where it is.
Sounds good to me.
We thank you for creating the Time and the Space for this discussion to be occurring. There is now a sense of a kind of a urgency we wish to impart about this material. There is the need to be doing this very frequently so that we can be completing. However, it must be completed if possible before the ending of this month of your time.

And so, we thank you.

Go as always with our blessing and our love until our next discussion.

For I am John

Notes.

Notes.

Chapter Six
Sound

And we bid you welcome. We are having another interesting discussion, are we not? What is your problem?

It keeps jumping forwards. We're supposed to be recording on track 4 and we're recording on track 6.

It does not matter. It is still the same kind of a situation. However, the number is very significant because it means you vibrating to the energy of the 6, which is far more conducive to having a good time.

But I wanted to vibrate to the number 4 because I'm a number 22.

Don't start, we're already in time.

If you vibrate to the 4 because you 22, you limiting your sense of Being. You not saying, "I know I'm 22. I will explore the 6 to see how it enhances." You saying, "I will utilise the 4 because I already know it is conducive to a good time." Do you see? So you become entrapped by the energy you seeking to explore. However, we already been talking about that for a lot of time, have we not?

Yes.

Do you notice we changing the scope of the energy?

(Referring to moving into a bigger space for the session.)

Yes.

So we gone into a bigger space of the Being, having a much larger kind of an energy to explore. It is very good, you know. That is because what we are going to talk about is very significant.

We been talking about your Time. We been talking about your Space. And of course you going to be having questions about it. However, we would prefer that you do not be asking your questions about Time and Space at this point of your time, in this space. Do you see?

OK.

Thank you very much. What we wishing to do is to take you beyond the energy of Time and Space and if you ask your questions about them, you are in it. Do you see?

Yes.

There will be an opportunity to be asking multiple questions about anything we been talking about. However, will not be at this point.

So, if you are in tune with Time, then you are creating Space, which in actual fact is consciousness. We are agreed upon this principle, are we not? Therefore, you are in a state of Being where you are connected to All That Is.

Well, what does it mean?

Because in your finite mind you cannot comprehend All That Is. And, with your finite mind, if you seek to understand it, you going to use words. Words bring you back to the 3rd dimension and so once again you stuck in it. And even in our explanation of it, we got to be using words to you. However, we are going to talk to you about how you can go beyond words.

Great.

You already been doing it.

Oh. Cool! Bring it to my consciousness, please.

Because you Sherrie the guinea pig for the whole situation. We been practising upon you. You Tony also been a guinea pig. However, we been practising on you in a different way, do you understand?

Squeak, squeak.

Very good sound.

(Laughter.) We need a video for this book.

That is becoming. You got to be doing this kind of a video

situation, you know, because for a lot of people simply to be listening to a voice is not sufficient. They like to be nosey. They want to see what is occurring; and because they can see, they feel they have a connection to the energy that is being expressed and so they are more open to it. What they are doing is that they are combining all of their senses in one. Do you see?

Yes.

However, that is another topic for another book.

Now, in order to be understanding this kind of a situation, you gone beyond Time, you gone beyond Space, so you are creating an opportunity where you are at one with All That Is in consciousness. We are agreed upon this point. However, you do not know how then you can work with All That Is because you cannot use words.

Words are 3rd dimensional limitation. So, how you going to do it? If you have the opportunity to connect to All That Is how are you going to understand your connection to All That Is? What is the key you can utilise or that is available to you to enable your consciousness to expand within All That Is and therefore be able to comprehend as a part not only of your Being but of the Being of every living entity? How you going to do it? What kind of a situation can you be doing?

Well, I've been sounding.

That is exactly the situation.

Yes, that's what it does.

The moment you emit sound, you stepping out of the limitation of Mind.

Yes, that's it.

Because Mind is able to function on many levels and can stimulate many levels of activity. So it's very important. It is

a vehicle to enable the sound to be emitted because it sends instructions to the body and the sound goes forth. However, Mind in and of itself does not create sound. It creates the mechanism to enable sound. It is a vehicle. Do you see?
Yes.

As a consequence, the moment you are sounding, you are sending forth your vibration into the world. So you are seeking to attune. And you will find that, as you sound, first of all you begin to release any limitations, any inhibitions, any uncertainties and particularly any emotions or judgments you been holding. The more that you do the sounding, however, you will find that the note changes. It at the same time becomes deeper and yet clearer. It almost sounds as though the sound is coming from somewhere else. It is you but not the you that you know.
Mmm.
Exactly the situation. You have experienced it have you not?
Yes. It's a bit bizarre.
Of course it's bizarre because your 3rd dimensional mind at that point says, "Oh, what is happening? I cannot understand it." Whilst you continue to sound your 3rd dimensional mind cannot control the situation. The moment you cease to sound in order to explore the bizarre energy of what is happening, you lost your connection to All That Is. You back in your mind and your 3rd dimensional concrete mind. Do you see?
Very good, yes!

So, the sounding goes forth. You are transmitting into your world your vibration, your energy. Not the physical form of who you be and its consciousness, the totality of your Being is being transmitted.
Well, that is all very well and good. You now have a connection to All That Is and you know you got a connection

because you telling it about it – you sending forth the sound. You are saying, "Hello everybody out there. This is who I Be." Well of course, some of those everybodys out there going to say, "Oh Lord, here we go again!" Because when you first doing your sounding, what begins to occur is that, as you move through the suppressions, the inhibitions, the restrictions within you that you are working upon, the sound is loud because there is the need of the force field of energy to expel. Not to express, to expel.

Well you know, you deafening everybody! All of the energy of All That Is vibrates in peace and tranquillity. Suddenly you got this raucous kind of a noise and it is broadcasting throughout the Universe.

Can you imagine what would occur if everybody sounding about the place?

However, as you become accustomed to this kind of a situation, you will find that you can sound very slowly, very quietly, equally as deeply and clearly. You can do it without actually emitting a sound.

You are not thinking about it in your head. That is a confusion. Sometimes you can think in here *(pointing to the head)*, 'Well this is what I doing." You are still transmitting a vibration. It is not a sound. It is a different frequency. You come from the heart of your Being and you sit in that heart and you **hear** that sound. You do not transmit it. You **hear** your sound and in hearing it you are transmitting it. So initially you got to have a physical kind of a situation to understand what it is you are doing. To begin to feel the rhythm of the task – there is your Time. To feel the Space you are creating for the task to be completed. And in so doing you connecting to All That Is because you gone beyond Time and Space.

Then you stand in consciousness of all and All That Is

together and the sound begins to change, to soften and to become harmonious. You feel as though every aspect of your Being is alive and at peace. You feel the expansion of every aspect of your Being as though you are transmitting not sound but Love. And it goes further, further, further. You do not have to blast it out into the Universe. It's going to do that automatically, do you see? And then you find there are occasions you need to be sounding and you cannot create what you been creating. You cannot move through the Time and the Space in a physical manner as you have been doing.

However, no matter the task you can be performing, you can feel the heart of your Being and hear your sound and you doing exactly the same situation, do you see? So you are hearing your own energy as though for the first time coming from the heart of your Being. Yo are at that point of your time, pure Spirit operating at a spiritual plane of consciousness. Do you understand?
Mmm.
Therefore, you feel very happy because you connected to the spiritual Essence of who you Be. You sounding, you are enhancing the energy of the whole. You are connected to All That Is. You feel the feel the peacefulness of knowing that you are in harmony with All That Is.
But there is still something missing.
What is the something missing? It is not complete. Why is it not complete?

I don't know.
Something to do with communicating it?
Well you are communicating. However, you not listening. When you are sounding you are listening to your own sound and its connection to All That Is so that is you giving forth your energy. That is the breathing out. At some point you

118

got to breathe in. If you do not breathe in, how can you hear All That Is in its desire to communicate with you for your growth and your expansion? Whilst you are only sounding, the communication is only going away from you. So at some point in that sounding, again you transcend Time and Space and you listen, not to your own sounding, you sit and you seek to listen to the sound of the Universes.

To the sounds of the different dimensional planes of Being, because each plane of Being has a different frequency. Obviously if they all had the same frequency you just simply go through one door into another. You do not. You got to lift your own frequency to move into those dimensions of Being.

So, in sitting and listening in that Space – and its got to be in that Space (if you not in that Space you not hearing the sounds of the dimensions) – you can hear the echoes but until you are in that Space of consciousness, you cannot hear the vibrations, the frequencies, the sounds, whatever terminology you wish to use, of those dimensions of Being. And once you hear those sounds and you attune to them, you can step into any dimension you wish because the sound opens the door. And away you go.

If however, you are sitting and you are hearing the sounds and you interpret the sounds, you closed the door. How could you interpret? Why would you interpret? What could be occurring to create such a situation?
So why would you be creating the need for interpretation?

So we can understand it? Control it? To bring it in? To communicate it? That's the mind thinking about it.

Exactly! That is what occurs. The moment you begin to seek to understand what it is you are experiencing you have stepped out of the Space, that consciousness, back into your 3rd dimensional reality. All you need to do is to sound and to hear sound during the experience itself. Once the experience is completed, then as you seek to understand – not to understand to comprehend because it is a different kind of a situation- once you seek to comprehend, then your 3rd dimensional mind, because it has had the experience, will in and of itself find *your* words to describe *your* experience.

You can then share it with others only, however, as *your* experience because theirs can and will be very different. What you are sharing is the technique, for their experience is their own. Do you see?
Yes.

And so as a consequence, sound is very important. If you therefore expand upon the concept of sound, sound is a note, a tone, is it not?
Mmm.

When you have a series of notes or tones together you call it in your world music because there is a melody, a rhythm. So there it is in Time because it has a rhythm. As the rhythm flows, the music itself goes into Space. Do you see? So music creates states of consciousness. If therefore you have very discordant, very heavy kind of musical notes put together, you have a very concrete consciousness. It takes you into a density of consciousness. It is very heavy. It is very hard to be moving. It is very hard to be joyful. Indeed, it is a consciousness of sorrow.

And if the beat is very fast, the rhythm is very fast; it takes you into anger.
Mmm.

If you have a very flowing kind of a musical rhythm, well,

you either going to dance depending upon the speed of the rhythm, the timing - do you notice in music, you talk about the timing?

Yes.

Well, the speed of the music, you either going to be dancing about the place or you going to be sitting and relaxing and going into peace, another state of consciousness.

Is that how music therapy is working?

That is so. It works upon all of the energy field. It is a means of creating consciousness so therefore it works on the total consciousness of the individual. Which is why it is so very important that those who are working with this energy understand what it is they are doing.

Yes because it could be dangerous.

It is dangerous. Because what they do is they have a technique they have been taught or they have been given, which gives to them an outcome. So they have a limitation. As we were saying earlier, you can have the technique and you can share it with someone. However, their experience is their own and is valid. So if you have a therapy of music, that says when you have completed this therapy you going to be totally well, you have placed a limitation upon this individual. The therapist has not stopped to consider what is the Karma of this individual. And if the Karma of the individual is that the disease within them, of the body or of the mind, is to create the death of this individual, the therapist, by stating that the therapy going to create wellness is setting up a very difficult karmic situation between the two.

The moment the individual recognises that there is no wellness going to occur, then the energy of that individual is no longer at peace. There is a feeling of anger, of betrayal, grief, a variety of emotions, which would not have been experienced, if the outcome had not been made so very clear. The soul of that individual in passing carries extra energy that it now has to return to be releasing.

That occurs if the therapist themselves are not in consciousness of what they are doing. If they are focused on Time, if they are focused on Space they are not connected to All That Is. They cannot be a truly healing agency in the life of another. However, there are no victims. So obviously the individual who is passing with a added burden of Karma, had opportunity to clarify at the beginning of the discussion with the therapist. "Are you absolutely certain or is this your hope? Do you know what is my karma? Well then your system can produce this. However, if my karma is to be passing away, then your system will alleviate my process."

The individual is then no longer in anger or sorrow because the individual did not have an expectation of an outcome. The individual had moved beyond Time, beyond Space because the individual was with the rhythm of the energy and the expanded consciousness that says, "I do not know everything. However, I going to connect to All That Is and whatever is to manifest will manifest." Do you understand? *Yes. Thanks, John.*

Is this clear in Light of all that we been saying? Can you see how, from the moment we began these talks we were building, one upon another, a layer of understanding?
Yes.

Because if we were to give to you this information without all that has gone previously you would have no frame of reference to go beyond. You would have no understanding of what it is we discussing because where are you beginning? And that is what occurs for certain individuals who have the ability to go beyond Time and Space. They access All That Is. They access Akashic records, for example. They read all about everything. Well, that is a nice euphemism. They know because they connected. They not reading anything. They come back to your Earth plane and what they say is, "Well, you know, this is what is happening on the 12th dimension; and on the 15th you got all of these Beings; and you got to connect to them."

They do not tell you what are the steps to get you to the Space where you can make your connection. They are so enthusiastic about what they have accessed that even though they bring it to the Earth plane, they do not retrace their steps to bring it back in full consciousness.
They do not reconnect to Space, reconnect to Time, reconnect to perception then to understanding and then to the belief system of those about them. That is manifestation. Do you see?
Mmm.
An explanation of manifestation. There are many. So, because they do not do it, they can bring to the Earth plane many beautiful messages of Love and of Wisdom. However, how often have you heard an individual say, "Well, you know, sounds very fine. However, what does it really mean?"
Yes.
"Sounds very beautiful, however, must be for a very specialist kind of a soul because I do not truly comprehend what is being said or how it can be possible." So therefore it is inconceivable to the very individual it is meant to be of assistance to.

As a consequence, that individual closes their consciousness to that truth because they cannot comprehend it. Very good to have all these beautiful experiences. However, if you become so very enthusiastic about it, so carried away by the joy of the experience that you leave your concrete mind behind when you return, how can you be sharing what you experienced? The concrete mind is important because it enables you to function in your physical world. When you make connection to All That Is you making connection to the highest Mind, if you will. However, you cannot bring that knowledge into your Earth plane unless you bring it through your concrete mind. It is the transformer and the interpreter.

So if you having difficulty with your mind it is because, somewhere within you, you are in denial of its purpose. Do you see?
Yes.

Now, lot of people who are spiritual say," I have this wonderful concept. However, I cannot communicate it. I do not know the words." Or "I have this concept. I can communicate it. However, I do not know how to convey the fullness of it." What is occurring is that at the point where the concept or the message, the point where they were connected to All That Is occurred, at that point they allowed the concrete mind to say, "This is too big."

So they touched the experience. Does this sound familiar?
Yes, very.
They touched the experience and ran away from it because their 3rd dimensional mind said, "This is too big."
Yes, that's so.

Nothing is too big, nothing. What you need to do is to allow yourself to touch the bigness of it and say, "This is truly wonderful. I simply going to enjoy the experience." You do not have to worry about how you going to describe it; how

you going to share it; because you cannot. It is your experience. So, what you do is you allow yourself to touch it, to feel it, to experience it. Only when you have returned can you then sit in your meditation and say," I have had the experience. Please help me to understand how to describe it." Do you see?
Yes, yes.

Is that where…? I'll use me as an example.
Please do because we are. Is very good.

(Laughter) Feeling that bigness, another part of where my mind will go concrete is well, now I need to go home and study that, or learn that and do that so that I can bring it into those aspects; and that is control.

That is the concrete mind. It is so very big it is saying, "I do not know enough about this to explain it."
Yes.
So, therefore, it will look for avenues to give to it the ability to do so. You do not need to do any of those kinds of things. Experience the experience for its own sake. Feel the totality of it so that you know what you are experiencing without knowing in words. Do you see? You are not defining or limiting. Only when you return and you have allowed the experience to settle within you in your meditative situation, then ask, "Please show me how to put this into a manner of explanation of my experience that I can share with other people." Your concrete mind will then say, "Oh well, I know the answer to this situation."

Is this where people are getting more confused with filling their mind with more and more knowledge when the power of their own mind is…a bit of what you're saying?

The power of their own mind is all of what we are saying. Not a bit of it.

Yes.

When you are filling your head with knowledge, you filling your head with knowledge. It is not wisdom. We have spoken of this before, have we not? Wisdom is knowledge and experience. You got to have the both. If you experience moving beyond Time and Space, you not only have the knowledge that you have done so; you have the experience which is converting the knowledge into the wisdom to be able to say to other people that this is a state of Being. "I have attained it because I did such and so." It is not theoretical; it is experiential. It is your wisdom.

And so, as we were saying at an earlier point, you can say to them, "This is the technique I was using. Perhaps you would care to be using the same technique. These were the areas of difficulty I encountered because of my concrete mind or because of my fear or whatever. You may or may not experience a similar situation. However, I am sharing it with you so that you know it is possible and will not then fear there is something lacking within you for these to be occurring. And when you are achieving this state of Being, do not try to analyse because you will leave it. Simply feel how it is feeling because you know, when it is time to cease experiencing, your own knowing will do so for you."

Mmm. The urge is back.

"You just gradually return to your physical body and your physical consciousness and then you can think about it. Then you can talk about it and explain and share."

So it is very important significance. Without sound, you never going to achieve it. Sound is the greatest assistance in creativity there is. What has begun to occur however is that because it has been recognised as beneficial, rather than sound music has been introduced. Music is very important. However, music, the combinations of the sounds, creates a different energy. Providing this is understood, "by combining these notes this is the state of awareness I wish to be connecting to", then your music enhances your experience. If it is not understood then you may feel disappointed because you not quite accessed or you may feel elated because you accessed more than you were intending to access. There is no certainty about it, do you see?

When you sounding, there is absolute certainty. What you will find, and you've done this with this channel and the other group, you were sounding your soul note. The more you sound, that is the note that comes deep and clear. Once you cleared away the layers that you getting rid of. Be very aware of how your soul note feels. It feels very different to any other note that you make. And be aware of the power because the soul note has the power of destruction not simply creation.

Now if you may recall, at the beginning of our gatherings, where everybody coming along to be listening to the channellings, at the very beginning we were talking then about transmission of energy; and how if you not in harmony you can blow hole through somebody. Well, you see, sound is how energy is transmitted.
When you are unconscious, you wish to be sending healing, the energy of the soul uses its sound, its note to transmit the healing. So the more you are in harmony with your soul being, the more potent is the energy you are transmitting and the less forceful because it is in tune with All That Is. It knows exactly how much to be transmitting at any given moment of your time.

It is very clever, is it not? So, do you have any question about it?

No.

I do.

Very good. What is your question?

When you were talking and asking us what was missing, and it was the listening to the Universe, I just want to bring that in here. Lately I've been listening to people, especially in Time and Space, and it's like I can't hear them or it's what are you really trying to say. The last week, especially being conscious about time, it's where are you? It's like I'm not seeing them. There's just this thing....

No, no, no. "Where are you?" is a very good question because they are not vibrating at the same frequency you vibrating at. It is not that you cannot see them. It is that they are using sound to hide themselves.

That's it, yes.

Do you see?

Yes, yes. Very good.

So when you are having such a experience, that is why you are saying, 'Where are you going?" This channel has had the same situation, do you see?

Yes.

The both of you are talking to people. Suddenly you hearing all of these sounds but you know they are not truth.

True sounds.

That individual has stepped out of the centre of the Being into the layers, which surround the Being. So asking the question, 'Where are you?" is very good because they are not in the centre of who they Be.

Oh, good because I thought that was Time, too. Is that so?

Well, there are…it is the Time which takes them out of the centre. They have become focused on the limitation of Time so they stepping out the centre of who they Be to be chasing this Time all about the place. Do you see? And then they can give to you all of the justifications why they not doing or being what they supposed to be doing or being because they got no Time to do or Be. Do you see?
Yes.
It's very clever. And then of course, when you say to them, "You know, perhaps it would be a good idea to give to yourself some Space and perhaps to be meditating about it," they will also tell you why they got no time to do so.
Because they are attached to the energy circulating in the layers of their Being, it has more relevance to them because within them they are sensing an important change. They are frightened of it so they step out of the centre of their Being where they know they will experience the change into the layers. They have had that a long time: it is a lot more comfortable. Do you see?
Yes, very good.

So in order for these ones to move beyond, they need Time and Space to do so. Trying to encourage them to step forward before the timing is appropriate will prevent them finding the Space. So the greatest gift you can give to another individual when you see that they are moving through something difficult is to say to them, "You know, I going to leave you alone. When you ready and you wish to talk to me about how you can move forward, please to do so. However, until that time I going to say nothing more about it."
If these ones come to you and say "You know, I'm stuck. I got this, I got that." You say to them, "Please to excuse me. When you ready to move out of it rather than to claim it, I

will talk to you. What you coming to talk to me about is claiming where you are stuck."

Oh, OK. Yes.

"I have no intention of assisting you to become more stuck because at a soul level you do not wish to be there, so please come to talk to me when you ready to move beyond it."

What is occurring in your world, you know, is that people very, very clever, very sneaky. They given all of these tools for personal development and the very first thing they do is they find out how they can make the tool another limitation. "Oh well, I got to stay where I am because…" And they will use all of the tools and techniques as a justification for where they are staying. Do you see?

Yes, I do.

So they can say, for example, "Well if this was meant to be it would be happening. It's not happening so obviously it's perfect for me to be where I am." The truth of the situation is it is not happening because they are not creating it. So obviously it is perfect for them to be where they are because they are not yet ready to create it but what they are affirming is that Spirit is saying that is it is not yet time for them to create it. Do you see?

Yes.

It is a very clever manipulation of energy. So does this answer your question?

Yes.

Thank you very much.

Have you got a question to be asking? You very quiet about it all. Why is this?

I don't feel quite here?

And why are you not quite here? This is very good, thank you. Why are you not quite here?

Why?
Because you have become a guinea pig?
I don't know. I'm having difficulty focusing, staying with it.
You are having difficulty staying with the energy because you are either still in Time or still in Space. You have not gone beyond, do you see?
I think I handed the questions over to Sherrie.
Indeed you did.
I think I ran out the other day. I used up my quota.
Indeed you did. However, you are being a very good example of exactly what it is we were talking about earlier, do you see?
If a physical, spiritual Being experiences a spiritual reality, returns and does not put it into practical terms, those that are being spoken to cannot understand it.
Oh, right, yes.
What we are saying to you is that you do understand everything that is being said to you. However, the sense of being discombobulated, we are creating it around you so that you can be a example in this context to share with your world. Because it is going to go into the book that you are not quite here.
I would not say discombobulated. I would more say disconnected.

Well, discombobulated is disconnected because when you discombobulated you bobbing about all over the place. You not connected to the centre of your Being so the energy is not calm. So it is merely a discussion of words. If you wish to use disconnected then we will work with disconnected. Disconnected means that at some point your consciousness is not connected to the overall consciousness and energy of which we are speaking.
Yes.

So therefore you are being a very good example of how, no matter what is said, if the individual is not vibrating at the same frequency, waste of time. Now our earlier example was of the teacher or the person exploring not being grounded. This is an example of the opposite. The individual is anchoring the energy but the person being spoken to is not grounded because if you were grounded you would not feel disconnected.

Mmm.

So we thank you for that and you can let go of the feeling of disconnection and everything very happy again.

We also got to say to you that you not finished with all your questions. There going to be some more you going to be asking, you know.

Indeed.

But they not going to be in this particular situation because you been the one playing about with the energy, do you see?

Yes.

So we thank you for being a very good guinea pig - that is the term?

Yes.

Your language is very strange. Guinea pig, for the example to be clear in the book itself. And you are another example because you understood perfectly what we were talking about because of your own experience do you see?

Yes.

You have been experiencing it. He has not.

Yes. Yes. I had a completely different experience.

So you could comprehend because of the experience. For him it's different. He not had that kind of a experience to be able to have a clear comprehension – or so he thinks.

Yes.

And yet other areas, he had the comprehension and you

did not. That is how energy works, do you see?

I was going to say when you talked about time last week and you gave that particular part of the message to me. I couldn't get it. Maybe I was feeling like ...I was a bit...

Exactly. Because it resonated with you, it touched an aspect of your Being. What happened was that your concrete mind focused on the aspect rather than the overall, so there was a disconnection.

Yes, I can relate.

And that is what has occurred here. An aspect of his Being has connected to what we talking about and the concrete mind is trying to grasp it. And this is where, we thank you very much, you are a very good example of knowledge without experience. If you have knowledge without experience, you simply got theory. Do you see?

Mmm. Yes.

So we are giving to you knowledge and because you not had the experience of what we talking about consciously, it is simply theoretical.

Yes.

It is difficult for (Sherrie) you to grasp because you have not had the knowing at a personal level. Whereas for you, (Tony) because you been playing with the energy, the knowledge is making sense of the experience so now you have the wisdom. Do you see where the experience is the most important? The knowledge in and of itself is insufficient.

Yes. It means nothing.

It means nothing. You can say, "I know. I know. I know." If you never done it, you do not know. You cannot know because you never done it. So we strayed a little bit from the point of sound. However, it was necessary as a point of consciousness explanation.

Yes.
Do you have any more questions?

I just have one question pop in. Maybe this is mine. So sound, to put it into daily life example, there's a lot of road rage, a lot of sounds. It's loud. It's noisy. The world's getting noisier. I find traffic is getting very fast, very noisy. There seems to be a lot of road rage because of that. Is that connected with sound? Could you give us an explanation with sound?

You used the terminology noise.
Yes.
Your world is becoming full of noise and depleted in sound. Do you see?
Yes.
Noise has no depth and clarity to it. It is like a kind of a static interference. We use your radio as a kind of example, if you not attuned to the station, you going to get a lot of noise, a lot of crackling energy.
Yes, too much noise.
The noise is becoming greater because the people are not attuned to who they be. So they cannot sound their soul sound deeply and clearly. And because they know there is something missing they try to fill the void with music. The music that they select is representative of the subconscious energy they are suppressing.

So in your road rage situation, the individual who is going to get very, very cranky, be violent is already simmering below the surface at the level of rage. That anger, that rage is simmering and being stimulated by the music because such an individual is not going to want to listen to peaceful, quiet music. They going to get impatient with it. Impatient because it is not feeding the rage. They will wish to have a fast...

Yes, boom, boom, boom.

Exactly. That kind of a music. Very heavy rhythm, very fast because that is feeding the rage. The moment someone performs an action that they feel is totally inappropriate up comes the rage and out comes the violence. For such a one, what is needed is to teach this one to sound. However, you got to talk this one into doing so because they so attached to their rage, their rage makes them feel alive even whilst they do not understand why they are always so angry and they judge it. Of course, the judgment creates the rage. The more that the rage is acted upon, the deeper the judgment, the more noise within their Being, the less they hear their soul sound the more there is rage and anger and judgment and violence. Do you see?

Yes.

So, if you wish to assist the children in your world, to change this pattern before it becomes entrenched within them, you teach them to sound. You do not teach them to sing. When you are teaching them to sing, you are teaching them to sing someone else's song and someone else's affirmations. You teach them to find their own sound and to make their own affirmations in alignment with the sound. And they are creating a centre for soul strength and soul joy, which will mean that when they are older, no matter the challenges and difficulties they encounter, they will sound and the challenge will become clear or the difficulty will disappear. Do you see?

Yes.

It is very, very important this kind of a situation. Sound used to be a day-to-day part of the lives of all of those in your world. Gradually it has become depleted. If you look at it, your religions use sound. They toll the bell. They call to Allah. They play the cymbal. It is all the same tone they are emitting, transmitting. They are broadcasting to the world. This is the vibration. It is calling you to God depending upon your kind of a philosophy. So the tone, for example, of a church bell is calling you to prayer. However, you go to pray and what you hear, the sound of the words, trying to be used to communicate God is not in accordance and harmony with the sound of the bell. So you say, "No point going to this place because it has not the energy I am seeking."

You call to your, we will use the example of your Islam, you got to bow and you got to pray to Mecca. Now that is very beautiful. That is also a call to prayer emitted by sounds. It is not one. There is a song, if you will, that is called. It is not truly a song, however, best way to describe it. When that sound, series of sounds, goes out those who follow that belief, that faith, prepare themselves for their prayer, their devotion. So they hear and what they receive is according to the sound being transmitted by the one giving forth the call. If the one giving forth the call has a sound that is a true soul sound of depth and clarity, all those who hear are going to follow the teaching, not the interpretation.

Ahh. Is that what Jesus meant in his parable?
Exactly. If however, the soul sound is being infiltrated by the layers of the individual, those who hear it are going to hear the interpretation not the teaching. Do you have any further...You looking very...
I need to sound
....out of Time and Space, do you see?
Yes, I know.

136

I have a question.

It is why we gave to you a bigger space in which to be talking to you about it. If we been doing this in the smaller space you would have felt overwhelmed by it. At least you got the illusion that you got space for the bigness of it, you know.

Yes.

Please to ask your question.

When Sherrie was talking about road rage, some of....a lot of the music that people have nowadays, a lot of the... when you hear a car go past you can't hear the music. All you can hear is the deep base. A lot of the radio/stereo systems you buy are sold with the selling point of the system being because it's got so much base. All you can hear is the thump, thump, thump even above the actual tune of the music. What sort of long-term effect is that going to have?

That is materiality. That deep base energy is connecting you to material reality, connecting you to being imprisoned in matter. So the more you are hearing it the more you are convinced that this is all you can have and experience; the more therefore you are feeling limited, imprisoned and you got to strike out at somebody. It is why the violence in your world escalated.

We would ask you to go 20 years of your time into the past.

Twenty?

Twenty. What was the energy at that time of the sound?

Early 80's, it was Pop. Yes, it was more bouncy, more...

And what was the energy of the people?

The same.

Going about having a good time, wanting to have a party, do you see?

137

Yes.

Perhaps having a little bit too much of substances, falling about all over the place, but not the anger.

No, that's right.

The moment the deep base note came in as a repetitive rhythm, (because that is the significance; it is not the deep base, it is the repetitive rhythm), what began to occur is that the people listening to it, without recognising it, being hit over the head each time by the rhythm.

That's what it feels like.

Their energy being suppressed. They being beaten.

That's what it sounds like.

Exactly! Because that is what is occurring. They are banging their heads. Indeed, we ask you ponder this, in their dancing what began to occur. They began to dance moving their head in time to the base as though they being hit. Do you see?

Mmm. And they call it head banging.

Exactly! Because that is what they doing. They are trying to beat their head centres where their connection to their God is into submission to the material reality. And they do not even know they doing it.

The violence that is occurring around your world is as a direct consequence of how your people and their consciousness has become more and more entrenched in matter. It has nothing to do with God. It has nothing to do with belief systems. It has everything to do with rage. The rage that says, "I am helpless in my circumstances. I got to find somebody more helpless than me because then in punishing them, I do not feel quite so helpless. Does this answer?

Yes but it raises another question.

138

Very good. You see now you are connected!

With the deep base in the music, the continual thump, I find it very depressing. It …I don't like it. I turn it off. And yet, if you were to sit with a drum and make a continual, repetitive, deep drumming sound, that's invigorating or it can be relaxing depending on the tempo. What's the difference?

The difference is that first of all the difference is in the rhythm of the base. In the music the deep base is the underlying rhythm of suppression. However, it is also opening the consciousness of the individual to the words that are being spoken. So you got the repetitive rhythm and then you got the words coming in as a affirmation because all of this kind of music talks about anger, or loss or grief, do you see?
Yes.
So the base is being used to open the consciousness and what is coming into the consciousness is heavy, dense, material energy.

When you working with a drum, you got a repetitive rhythm. It is not as deep as the deep base of the music. That is significant. So therefore the vibration is slightly different. More importantly, you are using the rhythm of the drum again to open the consciousness but you not being told how helpless you are when you do so. You are using the drum to open the consciousness to connect to All That Is.
Mmm. Yes.
Or you are using very quickly, very speedily to have a party; do you see, to be dancing? Indeed, we going to say this: when you and this channel were in the place of Hawaii you were playing with the drums.
Mmm.

That is because you were encouraged to do so as a group. Did you all feel that you better all go and jump from a cliff?
No.
What was the energy?
Joy.
Because?
It was all one. It was great!
It was joy because the individual who brought to you his drums showed you a rhythm.
Yes, he did.
And he also showed you that you could put any affirmation to that rhythm.
Yes.
And the one that came forth, telling somebody to be quiet fit the rhythm but was humorous. Was no rude energy, no anger.
No, he got to express his frustration.
Exactly so! Therefore he expressed a frustration in a humorous manner, lifted the energies of everybody and everybody having a good time, do you see? Does this answer your question?

Yes. And is it making a sound but leaving it to be experienced by the person without interpretation?

Exactly! Exactly the situation! You got to have the experience. So, for example, the two of you are having this experience now. We talking to both of you. During the course of this discussion both of you have experienced the same energy in completely different ways. Do you see?
Yes.
Both of you have learned and expanded your wisdom because you have experienced differently. So that is why you can be having a group of individuals. You can be giving

140

to them the same sound; we will use your drum, you banging your drum, group of people coming together with the same intent. If their intent is to have joy, then they going to dance. No matter the rhythm of the drum they will find the Space within the beat.

Yes.

That is going beyond Time and Space. They will find the Space within the beat and create the dance. If they are coming together to create war, the rhythm of the drum will again give them the opportunity to find the Space within it for the beat of war and they will march.

And if they come together for healing, within the space of the beat they will find the healing energy and that is what they will do. It is the intent for which the sound is being heard and transmitted that is more significant.

And so, do you have any other questions or can our intent be to stop sounding about the place and disappearing?

No, I have no other questions.

I do but that will be the next chapter.

Probably.

Because I've just got to the point where the sounding is stopping and I've worked with the intent. So do you want to clarify a little bit about intent?

No, because before you get to intent there is one other thing to be looking at and that is the colour.

Oh, yes.

So there is the topic of our next interaction, colour. Do you see? So we thank you for this discussion, monologue situation once again. We very happy that you been willing to allow this to be created because now we know we going to get this book finished. It is very good.

Go with our Blessing and our Love until we meet again.

For I am John.

Notes.

142

Chapter Seven
Colour

And so we continue our discussion, our interaction about how you move through the dimensions of your Being and how, as you do so, you integrating one to another until you come to the point where you got the totality of your Being in alignment. It is not a stage of being in tune. It is a stage of being aligned because you gone beyond the attunement. Do you see?
Mmm. Yes.
If you think about it, when you working with sound you going beyond memory. You are learning to recognise what is your own sound. If, when you sounding, you not in tune with all about you, which is what a melody creates, you are aligned with who you Be. Do you understand?
Yes.

Now, at what point are you letting go of the song? In all of this we been talking to you about integrating the physical, the emotional, the mental. You know as part of the initiatory experience at some point you got to get rid of the soul. The soul is no longer needed as a vehicle of expression. It is therefore dispersed. It has served its purpose.
Now, when are you going to be doing this? Do you do it when you completed the energy of the mental? Do you do it when you gone beyond Time? Do you complete it when you gone beyond Space? At what point do you release the soul?

I didn't know that you did, did you?
Yes. It would be when you… you would have to move through those stages. Through Space? Yes, it would have to be

through all of them.

That is so. You cannot remove the soul as a vehicle of expression, release it from being the intermediary between your Essence and your physical persona, personality whatever you want to call it, you cannot do any of this until you have transcended Space: because Space is consciousness. It is only when you find yourself in tune with consciousness of All That Is that you are able to recognise that you no longer need a vehicle as a intermediary between you and it because now you done it on your own.

So at that point, the soul is no longer necessary. And so, what you are doing then is you are dismantling a vehicle of expression. Do you see? If then you dismantle the vehicle of expression, the soul, what you got left?
Connection straight with the Monad.
How you going to know the quality of the connection with the Monadic Being? How you going to recognise the Monadic Being? Do you know?
No.
Now this a beep (referring to the answerphone connection ending), do you see?
Yes.
Beep, beep, beep, beep.
Pulsing.
Exactly, of your telephonic communication, beep, beep, beep, beep. What does it do? Drives everybody mad! Do you see?
(Laughs) Yes.
So pulsing is not the answer to how you recognise the Monad. That is a next discussion. It is colour. It has to be colour. Think about it.

144

If you do not have the physical form, if you no longer have the sensation that you achieve when you are connecting to your soul energy, you are meeting this Divine Spark of Being as though it were for the first time. So you got no intermediary of the soul to introduce you. To say, "This is your Divine Spark. This is who you are. Please to be meeting each other." Out of all of the Sparks of Light that resonate in All That Is, because do not forget yours is not the only one, how you going to recognise? It is through colour because colour has a vibration.

So therefore, for example, if your Divine Spark is vibrating at the colour pink you know immediately when you see all of the other colours, you do not wish to be going towards any of these energies; because that pink resonates within you. It is calling you. It is magnetising you to it.
There is an esoteric phrase. The call goes forth. Well the call goes forth from the Essence of your Being. Your guides, your teachers, your Masters are all means of assisting you to connect to the Essence of your Being. So the Master is often seen as the originator of the call because as a consequence, you connect. The true call goes from the Essence of your Being.
So you been drawn towards this Essence. However, you do not know what it is. We will presuppose that you never met this Essence before. Because those who have done so, already know that it is the colour, the vibration of the colour, and how to get there. We talking for those who not certain they ever done it before. Always good to do this first.

So you are magnetised towards this Essence. Gradually what occurs is you find yourself within the spectrum of Light that is pink. So there not a lot of people in groups of colours. We talking now about Light. Your Divine Essence is pure

Light. And it is vibrating in the spectrum of pink. Another one might be vibrating in the spectrum of green or of yellow or whatever. So you are drawn toward that spectrum of Light energy. Do you see?

Yes.

Now, how you going to know in that vibration which one is mutual?

I'm not sure.

How do you know which is yours?

You do not. What occurs is as you journey through this pink spectrum of energy you become aware of living energy, energies because there lot of them. You become aware of a kind of a pulsation but it is not a pulse. It is but not for the purposes of recognition. We talk about that on another discussion. You become aware of a kind of a pulse and you feel drawn to this particular energy, breathing energy of Light.

I was going to say, is it breath?

And you know, out of all of these breathing consciousnesses, that this is the consciousness that is most applicable to you. Because it is your own. When you journeying to visit your home, you been away, you been touring all over the place, gradually as you coming back to where you been living there becomes a sense of familiarity.

Yes.

As the sense of familiarity becomes stronger, there is a knowing that you are almost there. That same knowing operates. You coming closer, closer. You know you getting to that point of Divine Spark that is you. When you meet, you know you come home. You have come home to yourself, which is God or whatever terminology you care to use.

So now you find yourself connecting to who you Be as part of All That Is in that pink spectrum of energy of Light. You are now seeing yourself as a Light Being. That has a tremendous impact upon the consciousness when it is accessed for the first time. After that connection no longer when you return to the physical body can you accept limitation. You have had the experience of being pure Light, pure consciousness, connected to All That Is without limitation. When you return to your physical body, you know that if you wish to do or create nothing can inhibit because you got the connection to show you how.

Yes, I see.

So this is where you bring in the Power. It is the power of your God. You as an aspect of that God are calling forth your Divine Spark, your Essence of Being. We have talked about the difference between the Being and the nature on many occasions. You call in this Essence that is you: because you not got a soul any longer attaching you to the material plane saying that you got to keep reincarnating. So when you are taking on a physical body and you moved through the initiation, you released the soul energy, you bringing in the Divine Spark of your Being. You become a Personality with a capital P.

A Personality that is totally attuned and aligned to the Essence of the Being. There is no separation. There is no attachment in consciousness to the material plane. All of that has been redeemed. However, there is the ability to walk through the material plane observing, assisting and healing without becoming entrapped within it. You know how to move beyond it. So, the more you practise this kind of a connection, the easier it becomes for you as a personality (small p) in your world, to be living your life. Do you see? Gradually you going from this small p to this big P. Once you get to the big P then you got to think about, "Do I really wish to be part of this Earth plane energy at all?" The answer is yes because you are in service.

Only when you have gone beyond colour, when you understand it in all its meaning and have gone beyond it, will you recognise that you are not needing to incarnate upon your Earth plane in any way, for any means. However, that is something for another time. Is this clear?
Yes. Yes.
Is very good because both of you are awake.
We can change that.
You can indeed. You can indeed.
So, you become in tune with the rhythm of the timing of, for example, your meditation. You do not establish a time that has to be a limitation. You say to yourself, for example, "Each day of my time at approximately this time, I going to sit for my connection. I know, in order for me to function fully with my responsibilities upon the Earth plane, 20 minutes of my time is all the time that is available." (So therefore you are setting the boundary.) "I also know, however, that once I step into my meditation, I can step beyond Earth time. I can feel as though I been meditating for 24 years of my time, return to the Earth plane and only 20 of my minutes has moved forward." Do you see?
Yes.
Very good. So you setting your time frame in relationship to your Earth plane responsibilities. You connect to the rhythm of the meditative situation, which is the breath. What a coincidence that you align your breathing because you trying to connect to the breath of the whole of your life. Not simply the aspect you are living now. At that point, you move into the inner Space of your Being, which is the connection to All That Is. You take your consciousness within your physical Being and then move beyond it. That is transcending Space.

You do not go journeying about the place, for this purpose. So you go within, you are focused upon the rhythm of the task, upon the connection to the inner aspect of your Being. You feel as though suddenly you are in a vastness, a void of energy. You are in the Void of energy because a part of you still believes you got to pay attention to your physical body just in case it dies whilst you meditating! Do you see? *Mmm.*

What you do prior to entering your meditative situation is that you ask that your physical form be guarded whilst you are gone. And then you forget about it. Through the purpose of accessing the inner space, you move beyond your physical body. You vacate the body. There is still the Silver Cord attaching to the body so life breathing into it. You move beyond the body and you journey over the Void, or through the Void, whichever way you wish to be talking about it.

Now because you have transcended Time and Space, the Guardians of the Void will allow you to cross and leave. They will not sustain you within it. You will know that you have traversed the Void when you begin to see the colour of your Divine Essence flashing toward you. Shows you moving out of the Void in to the spectrum of consciousness of All That Is, wherein your own Divine Spark is residing. Then you make your connection. The two become one. You know nothing is ever going to change your mind about the reality of your Being. When you done that, then your Divine Spark can be showing to you situations, circumstances, whatever in your meditative condition to enable you to pay attention to the aspects of your learning that need to be resolved.

Not necessarily Karma, simply aspects of your learning about which you need clarification or resolution. Do you see?

149

Yes.

When you reach the point wherein your connection to this Divine spark is able to be maintained consistently, that is when the soul is discarded. You do not have to discard the soul, go journeying about the place looking for your Essence. You connect to your Essence, then you discard the soul. Even that is traumatic because it is a part of your consciousness that is no longer appropriate. So that is why, when you discard the soul, you feel as though you been crucified. You are literally having to cut away from you a part of your consciousness that has served you so well in this particular lifetime and sometimes over a period of lifetimes.

Now what does this have to do with colour as a whole? Learn to see people in terms of colour. If you are seeing them in terms of colour you are going beyond your mind. We not talking about looking at an individual's aura. We not talking about even asking them, "What is your Ray?" When you are looking at an individual, what is the predominant colour you sense about them at the heart of their Being?
That's seeing their God? Is that the symbology?
That is seeing who they Be. It is seeing where upon the spectrum of Light they are vibrating. Then you will begin to understand what is their purpose. According to the colour vibration so is the purpose of Being.

Can the personality influence that colour?

Of course. The personality's role, we talking about a small p, the personality's role is to shield the colour of the soul; to shield the colour of the Divine Spark; to protect it so that the individual may perform it's function without being too vulnerable. So what you do is you learn to recognise what is the personality colour. You attune to it. Do you understand? Then, as you feel the time is appropriate, and you got to be very careful because if you not careful you going to fall into what is called the black magic, you ask to be shown if it is for the highest good of yourself and the other, what is the soul colour; and then what is the Essence. You do not seek to see these colours without the permission of the individual you are seeking to observe.

If the colour comes from the lower range of the spectrum, then you can ask to be given a indication whether it is of a positive unevolved and evolving soul energy or whether it be of a black magic kind of a energy. In actual fact, in doing so, you are protecting yourself. You're being told where it is. You not touching the other, attracting attention, if it is a negative energy. It is going to be happily going about the place thinking it is unobserved. They not going to be bothering you because they think you going to be very nicely misled. Does this answer your question?
Mmm. I think so.
Do you wish to expand upon it?

Yes. Can the mood of the person affect that colour?
Only the colour of the personality. For example, you got your phrases in your language. Somebody being angry – they seeing red. So when you looking at the energy of the personality of somebody very angry, you going to see red. Depending upon the shading of the red, will tell you if the anger is destructive or constructive. The darker the colour, the more destructive the intent. It's murky, it's clouded, do you see?
Mmm.
Whereas the brighter the colour, the clearer the intent,

therefore construction is going to occur, even if something is destroyed in the process.
Yes.
If you see somebody who is a very envious individual, what colour do you think you going to see about them?
Well, green is the saying. If they're known as a...?
Jealous individual.
Green. A dark green.

Now think about it, anger is red. That person is seeing red. If you look at the energy of your Ray, it is power. It is will that is thwarted which creates the rage, the red. So it is the Ray 1 aspect of energy now being allowed expression. It does not mean the individual is a Ray 1 energy but it does mean the personality at that point is vibrating to that Ray. This is where there is a lot of confusion in your world, you know. "Oh well, if you angry person, you got to be Ray 1. "Not at all. You can be an angry person expressing through Ray 1. However, if you bossy person you got to be Ray 1. Do you see?
Mmm.
Now we bossy individual, however, we not Ray 1 we Ray 6 because we nice fellow! To be doing what we doing now, we are utilising the energy of that first Ray. When you green with jealousy, well the colour green is the colour of the heart centre. So if the energy of the heart centre is murky, you going to be jealous because you not having harmony in this place. Do you see?

As you aligning yourself to the harmony, the jealousy is going to disappear. If you very, very fearful people going to say that you are a coward. They talk about you having yellow, do they not? Look at your chakra energies do you see? The yellow is the colour of your solar plexus where the

152

thought that creates the fear originates.
What about orange? What about it?

I wish to talk about yellow?
Why do you wish to talk about yellow?
You've explained where the negative, the fear, the source of the thought for the fear comes from as in the terms of a coward.

That is so.

Can you... if you have someone opposite, the opposite to a coward is someone, if we take it in a fighting or violent situation, what about the person – I'm not saying it's right or wrong – who in case of a war or battle is doing what they think is right. You have the coward and you explained where the thought comes from. The opposite to the coward is someone prepared to get up and fight and to lead the charge, if you like.

You just answered it. Lead the charge.
Yes, so where does that thought come from?
That is not a thought.
What colour is that?
That is the red. The power to initiate, to begin.

OK. So where does the thought for that come from?
The thought is still within the solar plexus from the perspective of an absence of a thought of loss.
So all the thought comes from that same point?
Thought originates from the solar plexus. However, we better clarify because this can be confusing. When you have fear, fear is the predominant thought. It is not simply just the emotion. It is the predominant thought. If someone is truly

153

fearful, that thought governs who they Be and they accommodate their life according to that thought. Do you see?

So for example, if you have a fear of stepping into a vehicle and driving anywhere at all, you will be absolutely convinced that it is going to be detrimental to you. What you will do is you will spend all of your time thinking about how you can be getting about the place without having to step into your car.

That sort of fight or flight?

Not at all. Different situation. We talking about the mind. The mind is consumed by the fear. However, the fear originates in the thought that if I step into that vehicle I going to be losing my life or I going to be injured. No matter. So, the whole of the personality is governed by the mind continually seeking ways and means not to have to step into that vehicle to drive it.

Would be uncomfortable being a passenger but safer than driving because of the thought. The predominant energy being used is the energy of the solar plexus; because the thought driven fear is occupying the individual.

If you have a fight or flight syndrome there no thinking involved. It is an instinctive reaction as a consequence of an emotion.

Oh, all right. Yes.

And that is your orange. The orange steps between the two. If you have purified your base centre, if you feeling very strong in your sense of this is who you be, not necessarily strong in your idea of who you be, but physically. "I know I am strong fellow. I know I got very strong constitution." But you not altogether certain how you feel about yourself.

So you walking about the place and suddenly there is a

challenge to your sense of identity. "Who do you think you are?" Do you see? Now depending upon how strong is the red energy determines whether you fight. If however you not certain in your mind about who you are, you going to take flight. That is the orange. It is the bridge between the two, do you see?
Mmm.
Then once you know who you are and you comfortable about your value, then you got to go to the yellow. You see you moving through the colour spectrum. You got to go to the yellow because then you got to know in your mind who you are. Then if you challenged as you walking about the place, you know you can answer in one of three ways. You can either punch the fellow on the nose; or you can say, "let us have a discussion about it," which is your mind: or you can reassure this fellow because you responding not reacting. You moved beyond that vibration, do you see?

So you feel you knowing who you are and yet there is a part of you that feels jealousy or envy. Why? If you got red, orange, yellow in alignment or attunement, why would you feel envy? Surely this is impossible?

You're not in harmony with your soul? You said earlier it is to be in harmony?
It's personality.

The personality knows who it is with a little p. However, it has not aligned to the soul so, as a consequence, if it sees someone else appearing to be getting something that it is not getting, at that point it is out of alignment with the soul knowing of its purpose, of whether it is appropriate, even whether it actually needs whatever it is somebody else is getting. That's when you get this murky kind of a green

155

energy, which is always positive because in order to resolve it the personality got to talk to the soul.

So the soul can actually use such an emotion to stimulate connection. How often you see somebody want something somebody else got and when they got it they do not want it anymore. Because now they proved to themselves there is an equality. Has nothing to do with what the object is. It is feeling equal. Do you see?
Mmm.
The personality needs to feel equal and does not because it not connected to the soul at that point. Once it does, nothing else is of any significance, throw it away, not even interested. Do you understand?
Yes.

Of course, once you vibrate to this kind of a frequency, more and more you want to be communicating. Well, this is where you can get into all kinds of difficulties. Your sacral centre, which is the orange, as the bridge between the base and the solar plexus, is balanced by your heart centre. It is balanced only in the respect that the sacral is the mediator for the personality and the heart centre is the mediator for the soul. So these are the two that come together when you trying to align your soul and personality, do you see? However, when you start to be talking about the place, your throat centre needs to express at a personality level to the other personalities it meets. If you not aligned, these *(pointing to sacral and heart centres)* cannot express fully. You may feel very centred in your personality, very comfortable with who you Be at a personality level, not a soul level. Everything you talk about will come from the head. You will prove knowledge. Every time a feeling is discussed, you will discuss and analyse it because it keeps you safe.

When the heart, as the soul, has interacted with the personality, when you communicate you can communicate on many levels. You can talk emotionally. You can talk mentally. And you can and will talk spiritually. Unless of course, you got layers you still clearing, in which case you will not. However, we presupposing that you got no Karma, got no blockages. Even that expression, however, is the lower expression of the Higher Mind. Just as you have your sacral as the lower frequency of the heart, so the throat is the lower frequency of the intuition. Again, colour spectrum; only now you working within a very narrow spectrum of colour, from a blue to a dark blue; and then to a violet.

The spectrum is becoming smaller because you more and more aligned, you do not need to have this wide band of energy in the individual. Once you are communicating from the brow, which is the intuition, the transmission and reception of energy, then everything is in attunement and alignment. The crown vibrates fully and clearly and is wide open. At that point you can connect anywhere to anything in All That Is.

So, when you looking at an individual, sense what is the predominant colour. This is where you got to look at the colours they are wearing, because the personality will wear colour as camouflage. What is often seen as a obvious colour, has nothing to do with the true colour. That is where your people find that they falling over because they have taken the subconscious recognition of the colour energy and made assumptions. When the individual does not speak or act according to that colour, they fall over with surprise! Do you see?

Yes.

"Surely this is who you Be? How is it you not acting in this way?" Well, you know, this is the camouflage. It is the personality putting on a show, fulfilling its role, do you see? Do you have any questions about it?

Does the colour that you're wearing in your clothing…how does that affect you on a daily basis?

On a day-today basis, the colours that you wear indicate energy you are taking into yourself for one reason or another, as a consequence of how you are thinking or how you are feeling.

So is the colour opposite to how you are feeling or thinking? Or does the colour….?
Enhance. For example, first of all we clarify. If you find you have a predominant colour in your wardrobe, that predominant colour is a reflection of how you, as a personality, are seeing yourself.
Scary. (Looking at his multi coloured clothes!)
If you got multi coloured wardrobe, you see yourself at a personality level as a multi coloured individual. Why is that scary?

Well, people that have a lot of dark red, as you used that colour earlier, that's a refection of their personality.
They chose that within them. Their personality colour is red but they are vibrating at the red of anger because they not yet cleared.

Someone may have a very colourful kind of a wardrobe and yet only wear black. They do not know themselves and, more importantly, they are afraid to know themselves because they may discover something they do not wish to see. Does not have to mean there is anything negative about them. Usually nothing to do with negativity. It is because they are afraid of their own power.

Makes sense. Yes

So if there is a predominant colour running through the wardrobe energy, you know that this is the personality unconsciously demonstrating to the world what is its colour. If your personality is acting consciously it's going to have a lot of colours. Then it is difficult for anybody to know what is the appropriate colour. You see, that is the camouflage. That is the mask.

But with a predominant colour the personality is unaware consciously. Do you see? So therefore it is easily seen, recognised and understood: and can therefore be manipulated by others who have this kind of a understanding. When the personality becomes multicoloured, then what you do is that you observe the individual in the clothes they are wearing. You ask yourself, "What is the predominant energy emanating from this individual that I am sensing?" If the energy you sense resonates to the colour they are wearing, your interpretation of the colour they are wearing, then you know that that is a true refection of who they Be.

If the energy they are emanating bears little relationship to the colour they are wearing, you know it is a mask. They are using it as a disguise. Is this clear?

Yes, it is.

Then you can see the personality and you can see how it is trying to operate as a mask.

Now, when it comes to the soul energy, it has nothing to do with the clothes you are wearing. Has everything to do with how you are interacting with others. It is your connection, the colour of your connections, rather than the colour of your clothing. Now that is something to ponder, is it not?

Yes. So how do you assess that?
We use both of you as a example. If you had to describe
the colour of how you connect to people, your first
connection to an individual, what colour would you describe
it to be? Your very first connection.
I get the word blue in my head
Blue, what does blue mean?
I don't know. I'm blank, I just kept getting blue.
The reason you are blank is because you doing it without
fully understanding what it is you are doing so, of course
you blank. You cannot give the answer because you do not
consciously know the answer.
True.
Very good.

What would be the colour if we asked you how you connect?
Your first connection to people, what colour would you give
it?
Purple.
Why do you think it would be purple?
I don't think it's purple. I feel it's purple.
Why do you feel it's purple?

The first feeling that was there.

So both of you intuitively know the colour of your connection,
without necessarily understanding why.
Yes.

*I can only describe it as my own understanding of the energy
of different colours as it is at the moment.*
So what is it that purple represents?
*To me blue is a healing colour; generally speaking blue is a
healing colour. Purple to me, that end of the spectrum, is a*

healing colour but it's more towards the spiritual side, if that's the right word?

You are using your spiritual connection to make connection without necessarily knowing what is the purpose of the spiritual energy within the connection. That is why you see it as purple. That is exactly the situation.

Now with regard to the blue, if you recall earlier we talking about communication?

Mmm.

The lower and the higher. Your connection to people is a connection of communication. You want to know. Do you see?

Yes, exactly. I'm a sticky beak. (Laughing.)

You wish to know. So, because you wish to know, blue is the colour of your connection; you talk to people, they talk to you and you get to know. That is why it is blue. Of course there is healing. However, all of the colours bring healing.

Yes.

So the purple and the blue is healing, red is healing because red brings a kind of a vitality, a motivation. So that is a kind of a healing. If somebody got no motivation, that is a energy that brings motivation, brings healing.

Very good.

Of course, it's very good because it works.

So what's purple? Can I ask because I want to know? I'm sorry, Tony.

The purple energy is the spiritual connection but it is magic. So when this one connects to people he connects through the use of his magic, his spiritual magic to understand them. Not because he wants to know about them, but because his focus is the healing of the Earth.

Mmm.

If he can understand the people, then his magic can activate their magic and the Earth will be healed. Do you see?
Yes.

If you know about the people you are meeting, then through that interaction, through the discussion and the knowing, you then have a understanding. And through your understanding of them, you can show them how to heal. And through your understanding of them, you will heal yourself: as will he through the Earth magic, do you see? Do you see how it works?
Yes.
It is very sneaky, is it not? Is there another question about it?

No, but I've got this thought going through my head. Can you tell us what the colour beige means?
Beige is a non-energy. It has sufficient colour to have a semblance of life and indeed it does have life. Beige is a colour that is a combination of other colours. So it is not a clear stream of energy. If you feel that an individual is a beige kind of a colour, what you are seeing are the layers that individual is wearing as a consequence of a need to conform or feel part of something or someone else. It is a need of approval to give a validation of who they Be.
Does this make sense? Why are you so puzzled?
Because I'm wearing beige (laughing).
Then we ask you if this makes sense in your understanding of yourself?

I would say prior. At the moment I would say it's comfortable because I'm trying to understand me with what's going on.
So therefore, in order to understand yourself, first you got to allow yourself to sit in the layers that have made you who

you Be. Then you know what you need to do to discard them.
Mmm.

It is also a means of suppressing anything emotional that may bring discomfort or prevent you from completing. Whilst ever you doing that, you not suppressing a violence, you sort of calming it down, making it happy, so that you can continue the process. When you continued and finished the process, the beige will disappear. You going to be multi coloured personality again.
OK.
And that is what happens in your world. When an individual is going through a change they are toning down who they Be to be safe while they do it.
Yes, that's more like it.

It is exactly what you done. A part of you in this beige, the beige brings to your knowledge parts of you where you have accommodated, in order to feel accepted and loved.
Yes.
In order to remove those layers without reaction to what you discover, you got to wear the beige because the beige will help you to continue to accommodate only now you are accommodating your process.
Now I've got more understanding. Yes, yes.
When you done it, off will come the beige, on will come the red.

It's interesting. That's why I asked about the beige, talking about personality camouflage, because I have burgundy on underneath, which is a red.
However, the burgundy is a blue in the red.
Mmm. Yes.

It is a fear of your power.

Yes, that's what I got.

Your anger you experience at the fear of your power. A part of you knows you have this power and this connection. Now what occurs *(coughs)*, interesting we start to be coughing when we talking about your anger. You better do some more of those! *(referring to coughs)*

When you got a power, you know you got a power and you know you not expressing it, in order for you to be motivated to work with it, what you start to do is you start to see other people with their power and how they abuse it or misuse it.

Mmm.

You become aware of it. Makes you cranky. You have to become cranky because there is the energy of power in a anger to bring up the energy to make you begin to claim your own. However, because you not used to doing it, when you start to do it, you do it inappropriately, so that you have an excuse to criticise yourself so you stop doing it.

Mmm.

There you go. That is the answer to that question.

OK.

Does it clarify for you?

Yes. Yes, especially with the soul/personality.

Indeed because once you claim the power of who you Be, you will find you will be softer. It does not mean you are harsh now. You will be softer because part of your fear is that if you claim your power you going to be aggressive, or abusive. Yet you know you not going to be so but the fear is there. When you claim it fully, because it is an integral part of who you Be, and you feel attuned and aligned to it, your energy will be softer. There is no conflict. Do you have another question?

I'm not sure if it's a question or not. When we were younger, we were taught that the primary colours, there's two sets of primary colours; one is light and one's pigment. Yes?

That is so.
And they are different.
That is so. One is Spirit. One is matter.

Well, it's interesting. If you mix the three primary pigments you get black, material; and there's three light colours make white. So that represents the spirit form.
That is so. It is the Trinity in form: Father, Son and Holy Ghost. The qualities of Will and Power, Love and Intelligence. Well, you use willpower, conditional love and intelligence and you got pigment. Do you see?
Yes.
You use Will to Good, Unconditional Love and Spiritual Intelligence and you got Light. 'As above, so below.' The pigment shows the reflection in reverse if you will, of the Light. It shows what happens at the opposite focus of energy. When you working spiritually you working with Light, you going to create Light. If you work with matter you going to create black. It does not mean black is negative. Does this answer your statement?
It's just heavier. Yes.
Of course it's heavier. It is concrete energy. Light is energy that is not in a concrete form: matter is Light that has become concrete in its form.

So anything you see as black, anything materially you see as black, it means there is no light being reflected from it. It's absorbing all the Light.
That is so.
That's why it's black.

That is so. Has to do so.

If you are unknowing of who you Be, you going to wear black because you trying to bring in as much Light as possible to help to dispel the confusion. You do not wish to be radiating Light because you got confusion. If you radiating it, you never going to understand. So you wear the black to bring in all of the Light possible to help you through this unknowing. And once you got through it away you go again with your colourful energy.
Mmm. Yes.
Is there any other question?
No

So to return to the beginning of this discussion, once you transcended Time and Space, you become Light. In order to be differentiated Light, you become part of the spectrum, a colour in the spectrum of Light so that you can understand your energy. You as a individual in a physical body are still living. You need to feel a connection to who you Be. If you see it as a light, coloured light, it gives to you more sense of self, sense of understanding, sense of reality, do you see?
Yes.

If you can then see the colours of other individuals, it helps you to understand without judgment. Judgment is the single greatest inhibitor in your world. It helps you to see without judgment who this fellow is being and why this fellow is being. Once you have the understanding of yourself and those around you, you can breathe in unison with them. Once you breathe in unison with them, you both create a pulse of Light. That is another topic.
So do you feel we given you sufficient understanding?
Yes. Mmm.

166

Then we would suggest that in your meditative situation, you go through Time, through Space, into the Void, through the Void, into the colour of Light, see what is your colour so that you know who you Be finally – irrevocably know who you Be. The more you practise this the more you bring that consciousness into your Earth plane to enable you and those around you to go beyond it. It is healing. That is enlightenment because you bringing the Light of your Being fully and consciously into your 3rd dimensional body to radiate it into your world. Do you see?

Mmm.

Very well. Then we thank you for the opportunity to do little bit more of this material. We got another couple that got to be done. *(Laughter.)* Indeed always a little bit more. So we will say to you when you ready to do so we will be ready to do so.

As always go with our blessing and our love until we meet again.

For I am John.

Notes.

168

Chapter Eight
Karma

In our discussions, we now moving along very nicely. We talking about colour. That was when we were completing the process of elucidating, do you see?
Yes.
Very good word, elucidating.
Can we have some more clarity on that word?
That is exactly what it means, bringing light to a subject or clarification.

Now, there is an aspect to this colour that you need to be aware of. When we were speaking to you, we were talking to you about energy that is dark, energy that is light and the difference between the two. One other thing to be aware of is each colour has seven subdivisions of colour energy within it.
So, if you only looking at what is dark and what is light, you missing five nuances of energy, do you understand?
Yes.
Five nuances of energy because the vibration of the colour, if you will, will begin at the brightest of the energy, the lightest. As it steps down through the level, the energy becomes denser. The vibration becomes denser. In actual fact, the colour that you see with your physical vision is the densest level of the colour itself. And yet, even within that you have light and dark. 'As above, so below.' You always going to get it. No matter what you talking about, you always going to get it as a reflection.

So, it is necessary to understand that this is the situation with vibration because if you do not understand it through colour, which is a very good way, you both can see it, how

you going to understand your intent? It operates in the same way.
Ahh. Yes.
You got vibrational frequency of intent. Let us suppose that the intent vibrates at a balance between light and dark.

Can I interrupt you for a moment? Is this chapter of the book about intent? Last time we spoke there was to be one between colour and intent. So this one is about intent.
This one is about intent. There still got to be another chapter though, actually there got to be two more. Do you see?

Now we getting to this book. Colour not quite finished, which is why we talking about the seven planes. Intent not quite started because that is the next topic. But we got to introduce the concept at this point in time so we talking about intent without actually giving to you the chapter about intent.
OK. It's a bridge.
It is a bridge because we can show you lot of things to get there. Then there another chapter after that and then the final chapter you going to tie everything into pieces, do you see? We not going to do it. You going to do it.
With our questions?
With some questions, some observations and with some objections. Very good idea to have objections, do you see? Now, does this clarify for you? Does this answer your question?
Yes.
Are you quite happy about it?
Mmm. Yes.
Because if you not we got to give you spiritual clip upon your ear, do you see?
Mmm.

So, as we were saying, your colour has the seven layers of the definition of vibration within each colour. You got the planes of colour, just like you got the planes of expression or dimension, which is your Space. However, the colours do not vibrate to the planes of dimension at all. So, we only using it as though it were planes for you to see that there are bands to the colours do you see? In actual fact you got to turn it round. Colour comes into your world through a vertical energy, not a horizontal.

If the colour is coming from an aspect of the spectrum that is beyond the frequency of your Earth plane energy, it will enter the Earth plane at a tangent. Do you understand?
Can you run that by again?
Your Earth plane, because of its vibration, is only able to access a certain range in the spectrum of light colour. So if something from beyond that spectrum wishes to enter your Earth plane, it cannot come vertically. Your consciousness is such that it would exclude it. It has to come at a tangent. It has to come in at a angle to move through the layers to seed until the consciousness expands enough to see that extra colour. Do you see?
Oh, yes.

If you can understand this concept, you can understand that the intent in any energy must be understood from the concept of if it's coming from the highest or the lowest. If it's coming from the highest, how is it being grounded when it comes through the colour? It does not come through Space; it comes through the energy of colour. That is energy moving through Space, which is an intent, do you see? If you like, it's like a message from your God to you. It's got to come to you some way or another. It comes to you in colour. Once you got it, depending upon how good at receiving you are,

and depending upon the state of the frequency of your vibration, determines at what level of the colour your intent is formulated. Do you see?
Mmm.

Well, that's all very well and good. What does it mean? What it means is that therefore if you have a intent about something, just suppose you are a Messiah. Could be very interesting, you know. Just suppose you are a Messiah. You come to the Earth plane. You know what is your colour because we already spoken about it. You are aware of your colour; that is the energy you are wishing to share in your world. If however, in taking a physical form, because obviously you created it, you not yet purified that form of all of your Karma, well then your colour is going to be conditioned by your physical form, is it not? And its consciousness.
Mmm

As a consequence the purity of your message is not going to be clear. For example, you are giving your message as a dark blue energy. If it is a cloudy dark blue, lot of people going to get the wrong interpretation; going to go off at another tangent, which is the new colour coming in of the Messiah; going to go off at another tangent, create something totally different to what it was the Messiah coming to create. Do you see?
Yes.
It's not therefore the responsibility of the people. It is the responsibility of the Messiah, who created the situation before the energy was totally purified. Now, you going to say, "but surely a Messiah got to already be pure before they take a physical body?" Are you not?
Not now!

172

Common sense would say, "He got to be pure otherwise how could he be interested in this role?"
Yes, right.

Well, you know, if he was totally perfect, what kind of example would he be? Your day-to day people would say, "Well of course this Messiah can be doing all this because he already a very highly advanced kind of a fellow. We cannot hope to come near to this energy. Well, we better forget about it." So the individual has to have some energy that is not pure as a means to connect to those about the place for them to understand. That is why the intent comes with integrity but can be bewildered by the matter: the matter of the individual, the matter of the people.

Before we can talk about true intent, we got to talk about what is the bridge. The bridge is what has come to be known in your world as Karma. Now, why would we be discussing Karma when we been talking about colour and talking about intent.
How could Karma be the bridge between your colour and your intent?

Well, if you do a lot of actions, spoken words, it's not what you say. It's how you say it. If the intent is there it's not a negative thing. It's positive, good Karma, if you like. You can say the same thing with a different tone in your voice, a completely different intent and it's a very negative energy you're putting out.
Very good! We will use this analogy because in actual fact it assists in incorporating everything we been talking about with regard to sound, to colour and to Karma leading to intent.

The sound, the tone you are utilising, is the means of conveying what it is you wish to say. The colour of who you Be is the message you are conveying. If the gross material energy of your physical body is interfering with the colour of your Being, the sound you emit is not in alignment with the integrity of your Being: it is not in integrity. Therefore you are creating Karma because you going to have a negative reaction or response to what it is you talking about. Whereas if the gross physical matter is not clouding the sound and the colour of your Being, what you express will be in integrity with your Being and so therefore, however it is received by others, is going to be Karmically beneficial to the one speaking that truth. Do you see?
Yes.

It's quite a deep kind of a situation, is it not? It means you got to be aware of the Karma you creating every time you opening your mouth to be speaking. Now if everybody who believed they knew everything about spirituality reminded themselves of this small detail, do you know there would be a lot less noise in your world. There is a lot of babble about spirituality and unfortunately what is occurring is now you got a whole new series of rules and regulations that you got to conform with in order to be seen to be a light worker. Well, you know, we got to take issue with this phrase. Not one individual in your world is a light worker. Do you know why?
Is it the terminology? The definition of light worker?
That is so. What is a light worker, do you think?
Someone that works with Light.
That is so. Not one of the spiritual Beings currently calling themselves a light worker upon your planet is actually working with Light. They not bending it, they not shaping it, they not creating it, they not destroying it. What they are

174

working with and upon is their own Light Body and the Light Bodies of others. They are seeking to reconnect to their Being and in so doing the only way is to rebuild the Light Body, which was destroyed millennia ago, when the Temple was destroyed. Do you see?

Mmm.

They not light workers and they giving all of these rules and regulations about it. They are very many people who are quite happy to be following all of these rules and regulations. Does this mean therefore that it makes no Karma because everybody happy in the situation? Does it?

It depends on the interpretation, doesn't it? Different people interpret life differently, don't they?

It depends upon the intent of the individual who is proclaiming that they have the truth. The ones who follow, it depends upon the intent of these ones who are willing to receive the truth. So therefore to say, "This person is being a guru because they got a lot of wisdom; and these people following this guru because they wish to acquire wisdom" is not always necessarily true. This guru may wish to be a guru because this guru wishes to be worshipped. Nothing wrong with that. However, means that when this guru is going to heaven, as you would term it, this one not going to go to the spiritual planes. Why not?

That's not what he was intending. If the person's being a guru because they want to be a guru, not for the benefit, not from an altruistic point of view, they would have made the intent of doing it.... The intent behind the reason for doing it isn't the key to open the door to heaven.

That is so. What they are wanting, and receiving, is what is called glamour. They are feeding themselves emotionally. They wish to be worshipped. They being worshipped. They

175

very happy. As a consequence of being very happy, they are then happy to be beneficial to all of those about them. And they are, even when they being cranky about it, they being beneficial to those who are following them.

Now, the ones who are following are choosing to follow this guru kind of a energy because they don't wish to take responsibility for their own journey. So, what they say is, "Oh, I do not know enough. I very sorry, I am a pathetic kind of a individual. I give to you all of my adoration. Please show me how to live my life." And they do, do you see? This fellow is giving to that fellow a mutual exchange of energy. So there is no Karma. There is no karma of a negative or a positive. At that point it is mutual. At the point of coming together, the energy is a mutual exchange so the Karma is neutral. It is what is done with the energy that determines the kind of a Karmic ledger. Do you see?
Mmm.
Quite often what occurs is that the guru who wished to be helping others because it felt good to be needed, gradually becomes so used to being needed that any opportunity where someone who is a follower questions becomes a threat. At that point the guru uses his or her spiritual power with these followers to punish. At that point, you got Karma.

You may have a follower who may be very happy following a guru and reaching a point where suddenly the follower says, "I worship you all of these years of my time. Now I wish you to create this miracle for me." And the guru says, "I very sorry. I cannot." The follower says, "Therefore, I finish with you. I not going to be part of your organization any longer." That follower leaves and begins then to be speaking untruths about this guru; expressing anger, which is true, but telling stories about things that are not true in order to punish this one for what is a perceived failure.

Who carries the Karma?

The one with the intent to harm.

Who carries the Karma?

The one that did it for self gain?

Both. Both because initially the guru was quite happy to be receiving this adoration and therefore leading this one to believe that anything was possible by this guru, in return for this adoration. The follower because the moment he cannot receive what it is he wishes, he then got to punish: both of them because they speaking as though they following a spiritual enlightenment and they doing nothing at all that is spiritually enlightening or neither would be in that situation. Do you see?

Mmm.

Therefore when you are incarnating, even though you have an intent for the life you are choosing to live. Above and beyond that intent there must be attention focused upon Karma and its resolution or the intent becomes clouded like the colour becomes cloudy. The physical body carries the colour. This is how an intent in Spirit can become clouded when you take a physical body, do you see?

Mmm.

Your body elemental is carrying the knowledge of what it is you choosing to do; it got your blueprint. It's also got all of the challenges you got to overcome in order to do it. So the moment you try to circumvent your body elemental, what it does it to pop up and say that you cannot go this way because you got to do this first. If you choose not to address your Karma., if you choose to push ahead as a spiritual Being without recognising what are the Karmic lessons you came to learn and the debts you have to discharge to others, if you not willing to pay attention to this you are going to fall

177

into confusion. You are going to fall into error. You are going to fall into power, negative or positive, because both are the expression or manifestation of misused Karmic understanding. Your mission cannot be completed. It will be compromised. You may achieve but you will not complete.

So, those who do not claim their power are creating a Karmic debt. Those who claim it too strongly are also creating a Karmic debt. Those who do not work upon the issues of who they Be as a spiritual Being create a Karmic debt. What about the masses of people who have not bothered about spirituality, or have not heard of it, or do not care about it? What is going to happen to them? Are they going to have a lot of Karma?
No.
Exactly the situation. They not going to have a lot of Karma because whether you are conscious or unconscious is irrelevant. What is relevant is the intent with which you perform any activity and the opportunities that are presented to you to address Karma that are ignored. Whether you know them because you are unaware spiritually is not the issue. If you given an opportunity to change a pattern and you stubbornly persist in repeating the pattern, there is the intent, is Karma. If you know you got a issue to be dealing with and you not dealing with it for whatever reason, is Karma. Knowledge or lack of it is irrelevant. It is the way that you work with the intent, do you see?
Mmm.

Each individual incarnates with quite a few beneficial aspects of their Karmic life, presupposing they got them. Sometimes they do not got them, do you see? They will also incarnate with two periods of Karma. One is old Karma that they either been trying to resolve, found too difficult

and decided to wait for period of other lifetimes; or something that they connecting to finally in this particular lifetime for the first time. Second is Karma that is very, very recent, which gives opportunity to prevent this energy from becoming so entrenched in this individual soul that it becomes very difficult to remove. Do you see? That is why you got the two. So, you always got an opportunity to be clearing away this kind of a garbage as you going about the place. Because you also got the things that you done beneficially, for the good of others, to assist you in this clearing process you know you got a very good opportunity to be moving forward very speedily. Do you see?
Mmm.

What occurs is that when you take a physical form, as you growing, you attach to the form more and more as reality and your knowing is silenced. Because it's silenced you go through certain experiences. Not a problem. However, there always comes points in the life of the individual where they given the opportunity to re-evaluate and make change. Now if the individual does not understand the first opportunity, just simply that it's a strange thing to be occurring, then another opportunity is presented much more specifically for the individual to say, "Well, that's funny because I had a similar kind of a situation." This is to make the individual think. If the individual, on the first occasion, recognises and realises that there is something deeper and begins to work upon the understanding of it, that individual at that point connects fully in consciousness to the Karma.

Therefore the beneficial Karma can begin to have an impact in the life. Not just the negative. There is a lot of attention focused upon negative Karma but there is not quite as much as there is beneficial, you know.

Yes. Interesting.

So, the individual begins to work upon this knowing, this understanding. Begins to see a bigger picture and recognises where they are within it. Depends on the frame of reference of course, whether they begin to see themselves within this picture. If they then say, "That is too difficult. I am not going to do that." And walk away from it, what have they done?

Created more.

Blown it.

They have created the need to reincarnate to do so again under more difficult circumstances or, always remember this, they create another situation, *in the same life,* that is more difficult in an attempt to bring them back to resolving that lifetime.

Now what about the one who's oblivious? They totally oblivious about the first occasion, no Karma because they not been awakened. When the second occasion occurs and is more specific, and they begin to wonder about it, then they are opening the door to their Karma. However, until they begin to comprehend there is a deeper meaning, the Karma still does not operate. Do you see?

Yes.

Once they begin to see there must be some significance, to question God, to question who they are the door opens completely. Depending upon the quality of the lives that have been lived, so the Karma rolls over the individual. It either lifts that individual up or flattens that individual. Then they got all of that to be working through at the same time that they suddenly recognising, "Oh my goodness. There are a lot of things about this situation."

Now, that is simply connecting to Karma. In and of itself it is simply an event, which enables the individual either to release some of it or to add little bit more. Once you are aware there is more, it is your intent with regard to the awareness that is of significance. If you say, "Oh well, I got this Karma. I better clear it because then I can go to Heaven," well you not going to get there. Why not?

Because you're doing that event solely to clear the Karma. You like to be doing it to benefit. It's like your guru. It gives you sense of self-satisfaction in the physical and the belief that then you going to go to Heaven. Do you see? What about if you say, "Well, I got this Karma. However, I know I can be reincarnating lot of lifetimes. So what I going to do is to say that I very sorry I carrying all of this. I going to be as good as I can possibly be for the remainder of this lifetime to earn some more beneficial Karma. But I not going to deal with this Karma until another lifetime because it's too heavy." What is going to occur?
You're deferring. That person is deferring what he thought was the difficult aspect. He's deferring that and taking the easy way or doing the lesser, the less important.

That is so. Is like your money. Now just suppose you want to purchase something but you do not have the cash money to do so. So you say to this individual, "I pay you later." This individual says is a very good idea and is quite happy about it. However, what do they do?
Charge interest.

Exactly the situation. You got to pay interest upon it because what they saying is that you owe this to them. "You having this pleasure but you not paying me for this pleasure so I going to charge you little bit extra." Karma does exactly the same. Yes, you will build your points of beneficial Karma during that period. That is still going to apply.

However, when you come to meet the Karma you are avoiding, it's going to be harder. The hardness of it is going to outweigh the benefit you think you accrued. What occurs is that at the end of the life when you judge yourself, you will say, "I did this and it was the easy opportunity. The next time I going to make certain I have no opportunity to get away from it." Do you see?

So, at a personality level, it seems like a good arrangement. However, when you passing away from the physical, "Oh dear. I had a good opportunity. I missed it. I got to make sure that I do not do this again."

What would be the only, in this manner, appropriate way of approaching Karma?
From what point of view? What do you mean when you say "approaching Karma"?

For the individual.
I would think that to deal with it as it comes along. Because as it comes along in your life it already has its own....It already has been prioritised. The best thing to do would be to take it as it comes along and not prioritise it from a personality point of view. And I think from a general point of view of external Karma, let's say Karma with other people, that's purely down to intent. You would have to look at, "Why are they doing this?" You'd question yourself and come up with your own reason, your own motive. That it's for you and only you to pass judgment on your own reason, the individual's reason.

That is so. The moment that you become aware that you got Karma, if you then try to understand what is the sum total of this Karma, what are all the things you got to do,

you facing an outcome, not a process. Do you see?
Yes.
You are facing what?
You are facing an outcome not a process.
Oh, I see. Sorry.

So you detach from the need to complete and exactly what it is you say. You take each piece as it arrives; do the best that you possible can. When you feel that you have looked at this situation, looked at it from all different perspectives and done only what you believe to be in the highest good of all concerned, then you surrender it and move on. Do not continually revisit it. If you continually revisit it, you are creating more Karma.
Why? Why are you creating more Karma?

Because you're interrupting, again you're taking it out of order of priority. Instead of going 1, 2, 3, 4, you're going 1, 1, 1, and 1.
That is so. You're creating a blockage to your path. And whether you are aware of it or not, each time you revisit you form a judgment about what you already been or what you already done. Well, each of those judgments at some point have to be met and integrated. Karma is Law of Cause and Effect.
It is not an individual recording every misdeed you ever done, waiting with glee to punish you for it. It is a law of energy. It has nothing to do with individuals. It has everything to do with the energy of the individuals. Do you see? Do you understand?
Mmm.

Therefore the energy you transmit will return to you in one lifetime or another for you to reclaim, to redeem. You may transmit love. "I going to send love to the world." If the intent within you, not even perhaps acknowledged to yourself, is that, 'I going to send love because then I will be a loving person" You got Karma. "I going to send love because then others will see I am loving and love me." You got Karma. If you say to yourself, "Well, I can assess this individual. This is what this individual needs. I going to give it to this individual because it's going to make the path between us easier." You got Karma. Do you see?

Indeed.

Because your intent is to use and abuse. Your intent is to take advantage of your knowledge to seek an outcome. Those who are powerful or are claiming their power know within themselves whether they are using or abusing it. Those who are afraid to claim their power, judge those who have. Whether they are using it or abusing it is irrelevant. They will be judged because the one who has not claimed is afraid of their power and therefore places a judgment upon others to validate their refusal to claim it. Do you see?

Mmm. Yes.

So, does this mean claiming of power is a Karmic trap?

Trap? I don't know.

Indeed because it creates a lot of Karma when you claiming your power.

It's Karmic but it's not a Karmic trap.

How do you feel about it?

It's intent.

What is intent?

It would be their intent in claiming their power.

Not at all. It is about judgment. Karma comes from judgment of an intent. That is why we not going to talk fully about intent until the next coming together. Karma is about the judgment of an intent. And indeed is about the reception of the intent of another and the judgment of it. Do you see?

That is why power in and of itself is not a trap. Judgment is.

Do you have any questions about it? Anything you need to be asking about this situation?

Yes. Why is it in this session that Sherrie and I both feel so tired? Do you feel...?
No.
You don't? Well, why is it that I feel so tired, not now. Twenty minutes ago I could have fallen off the chair and gone to sleep. I had a real struggle to stay awake.
Why do you think that is?
I don't know. That's why I'm asking.
We would ask you to ask yourself why do you think that was occurring? There is a reason for this interaction.

Oh, for sure. I've had to close my eyes to listen to it.
Mmm. I did at first. I found closing my eyes I absorbed it better but then it was very close to the edge.
I know that I do listen, I do absorb better when I'm asleep.

That is quite so. Indeed it is accurate. Many individuals absorb information better when their conscious mind is otherwise occupied because then there can be no resistance to the information. In the same manner, when you closing your eyes to be listening to anything, what you seeking to do is to close out any distraction of energy that prevents your ability to hear, to concentrate, to recognise. That is all. If you had been falling asleep you would still have heard everything we got to say. You would just be a bit cranky about it because you did not consciously hear it that is all.
We wouldn't be able to ask questions either.
That is so. We would have to give to you spiritual clip upon

your ear to waken you to do so. So, does this answer your question?

Sort of.

What is lacking?

A direct answer.

You were given.

I feel as if within the answer you've given me all the pieces of a jigsaw puzzle but I've got to put it together.

You were given a direct answer. What you were not given was a judgment about falling asleep.

OK. I'll listen to it again.

Please do so. Any questions about it?

Can you briefly summarise the relationship between Karma and colour?

Not briefly.

We can however give to you some kind of a correspondence. You got a repetitive pattern of Karma, for example, lifetime after lifetime you been doing the same kind of a energy. You had the opportunities to heal it and you instead perpetuated the pattern. Then what occurs is the colour becomes denser and denser within your Being. Now, if your soul colour is dense because you carrying this Karma, you may choose to take a light physical body, colour of light, remember we talking about the personality as a different colour, a light, physical body personality because then it's going to reflect the light away from the density and still not going to be addressed. As a kind of a protective mask to hide the darkness within. And if you think about it that is often what occurs in your world, is it not? You see these people, very charming, very happy, very light and suddenly you find they been committing all kinds of atrocities. That is how it occurs.

Reminds me of a phrase 'blinded by the light'.

That is so. You cannot see beyond it. In actual fact, it has no true substance.

When you got a lot of good Karma, then that energy shines from within your Being through the gross material matter. When you are striving with integrity to improve, to heal, to move forward, your physical personality energy may seem to be dark. And yet the Light within shines through. So, as a consequence, you will magnetise to you Light in all forms to assist you on your journey. Do you see?
Yes.
When you reach a certain point whereby the soul is no longer needed, then you are standing in your Light body. You still having Personality with a capital P because it is the quality, the archetype of energy you are choosing to be wearing, to be part of as the mask for what you doing in unison with the Monad or the Essence of who you Be. So now what you done is you purified your nature and your Being is operating in your world. There is a radiance about that Being. Your Personality may seem to be light and it is true Light. It warms others. It is not so blinding. It is a glow that warms and uplifts others. The radiance of your Being begins to be observed about the head centres because that is where you are purifying your intent. It is coming from pure Love. That is why in your depictions of saints, they appear to be having this kind of a halo energy about their head. It is the radiance of their energy being seen etherically and portrayed, do you see?

So, the darker the colour that you working with, and we not talking about dark as in the spectrum of light to dark, we talking about cloudy, murky colour. You can have a very deep indigo colour and it can be the pure Essence. If it's a cloudy energy then you know you got a lot of Karma that is being held within that colour; either to be redeemed or to be repeated in another lifetime. The brighter the colour, the purer the energy, do you see? Does this answer your question?

Yes. OK.

Then we thank you. Is there another question?

Not from me. No.

Do you see the connection between colour, sound, and Karma as the bridge?

Karma, if it is unaddressed, can become in and of itself a closed door. It is impossible then for the individual to access who they Be, do you see?

Mmm.

It is as though the door has been closed. The key to lock has been thrown away and the Karma standing in front of it. Although the soul may be able to send some faint kind of idea of its colour to the individual aspect of soul incarnating, it is weak because of the weight of the Karma that is beyond the door.

If you see an individual who is struggling or floundering, if you have a means to assist and you withhold that means, instantly you have acquired Karma. Why is this?

Your refusal to assist can break the pattern. It could have been a pre-arranged event where the person is experiencing difficulty and you have the ability to help. So, if a pattern or arrangement has been made for you to be there at that point in time to assist that soul and its lesson and you refuse to help, it means that soul isn't going to learn that lesson it set out to learn.

That could be so. It could be that the coming together is for you to learn a lesson about assistance. The point is, however, that if you have the recognition of an individual drowning and you have the means of assistance, however slight those means might be, your refusal to offer help to this individual stems from judgment.

Mmm.

Either a judgment of the situation in which the individual is standing or a judgment of the individual. If you detach and say, "Well, I can see this. I not going to get involved." You already are because the refusal to step forward with a positive flow of energy means there is a negative judgment behind your detachment and refusal. Do you see?

Mmm.

It may not be obvious. It may be very subtle but it is there. If you standing in unconditional Love, you would offer the opportunity to that individual. You would say to them, "I have a piece of information, a technique that might be of assistance to you. If you wish my assistance please to make connection." We already talked about it.

If you withhold that information, if you withhold that stepping forward and connection, Karmic residue devolves upon you. It is dependent upon the extent of the outcome for the individual as to the extent of your Karma. If you know even a small piece of understanding and you do not speak about it, you do not say to this one, "If you wish to be speaking about it I have this glimmer of a understanding. Perhaps you may wish to be talking to me about it." And that individual continues and falls deeper, and deeper, and deeper into the situation, the deeper the individual falls the greater your Karmic responsibility.

Even though your piece of information might have been slight, it could have been sufficient to deflect that individual away from that path and into a different path, more suited.

Your refusal to offer is your Karma. If the individual refuses to discuss, that is theirs. But, if you withhold that hand of assistance, the outcome of the individual falls upon your shoulders. Do you see?

So we've got the difference between detachment to let someone...you'd have to understand the Karma, which was set in the colour each person brought.

Not at all.

What you do is you can say to an individual, "I can see there is a situation. If you wish to discuss, please to talk to me about it." Without going into the colour at that point. You are simply letting them know you are aware of their difficulty. You are not stepping forward saying, "This is your problem. This is what you want to do about it." You letting them know you are aware. If that individual comes to you, then you step into the colour and use the colour to assist them in what it is they need to understand at a Karmic level. Do you see? Detachment is not a refusal to offer assistance. Detachment means that you do not step into the emotion of what is occurring around that individual or a judgment of what is occurring around that individual. Do you see?

Mmm.

Does this clarify for you?

Mmm.

So if you know and you say nothing, is your Karma. Not for the answer, we not speaking about that. We speaking about offering assistance. The refusal to offer assistance is Karmic. It is always based upon a belief or a judgment about either the individual or the situation. And it is those, which create the Karma. Is there anything else you wish to be asking?

No. Not at this point.

Do you feel clear about what it is we been sharing with you?

Yes. Bits and pieces.

Does it make sense?

Mmm.

Good. Now we can be going away, allowing the energy to be working within you. If you feel bit confused about it, however, please be asking us. We be quite happy to be offering to you some advice or technique about it for your journey. Do you understand?

Mmm.

That is because we being smart! We just been giving to you a example of what we been asking you to do for other people, do you see?

So, that is all we got to say about it. In our next interaction we definitely going to be talking about intent on all levels of your Being. So be good idea for you to be intent upon what we talking about, and we going to be intent upon what we going to convey to you. The colours of your energy fields have shifted and changed. That is good because the energy of Karma within you is being resurrected.

That was a question I wanted to ask.

Which is?

Well I didn't know whether that would come out. It's about resurrection, soul and Karma. Perhaps that will go in the question book?

Good question for later. Please to make note of it because quite a lengthy answer. However, we been touching upon it as we been talking to you, do you see?

Yes, that's what I'm trying......

Certainly when we talking about intent, there going to be a connection at that point. However, in the final questioning, then you can be really asking about it.

So, we got two more aspects to be discussing. One is the

aspect of intent. Now what do you think the last aspect could be?

The resurrection?

Not at all.

Will in Action? God in Action? Putting all that into action?

Which comes under a kind of a heading of Power. The Will to Good.

So it's a sort of a conclusion to everything, isn't it?

That is so. And the final kind of a chapter is going to be questionings about what we been talking about for further clarification so we can complete this particular work in order to be beginning the next. Do you see? Now we begun we got a lot of information we got to be talking about.

Will Tony and I in some point of our questions and answers be able to give an example? As two people who've been listening to what you've been teaching throughout the book? Sorry to have thrown you in there, Tony.

I'm not sure I know what you mean?

I just feel that having the experiential by the time it gets to the Will to Good there may be a recognition or something where we tie up a little bit of personal to that as well. Am I being clear enough? Something practical to share as in how our lives have been. Not a big story just to be able to show the shift..

What you really mean is will you be able to provide the experience to be aligned with the theory we been sharing so that the book actually contains wisdom.

Yes. So Tony and I can say that here is a little story about it.

That is so. So you better be doing your homeworking about it, do you see? Otherwise you not going to be able to complete the examination. Very good idea!

We can make it. We've gone through it anyway.

We'll cheat.

You can try. So, we thank you for the opportunity once again.

As always you going with our Blessing and our Love till we meeting you again.

For I am John

Notes.

Notes.

Chapter Nine
Intent.

And so, we are now coming to that point of intent. We been building up to this over the past few sessions of your time. Now we going to be talking to you about it.

Intent is a very, very important aspect of any kind of spiritual growth, any kind of spiritual work, any kind of spiritual living. You can be spiritually active without working, or without even being conscious that you are developing spiritually. You simply live spiritually. The intent is necessary, obviously, because if you do not have a intent, you going to be bobbing about all over the place, are you not? You going to be discombobulated. First you going to be here, then you going to be there, then you going to be here again.

Those who are seen to be kind of a butterfly energy, whether it be spiritually or socially, are those who have not formulated an intent for that part of their life. So what they doing, they flitting about all over the place trying to find out where they want to be, if they know where they want to be. Do you see?

Mmm.

And they touch, and they sense and then feel it is too much or they got enough of what it is and away they go again; to another touching, feeling moving on. So therefore, are they wasting their time?

No.

Why are they not wasting their time?

Because maybe in doing that they'll find what it is they looking for?

I don't feel it's a waste of time because they're going to find

195

something about themselves anyway.

They may or they may not, depending upon how open they are. However, their presence is having an impact upon the groups they connecting to: kind of as though they pollinating these groups with the aspect of who they be that the group can either contemplate or reject. Whatever, there is a change of consciousness because of their presence. So even without an intent, there is always an outcome of growth and learning.

However, intent creates the ability to focus, to have a consciousness about what is occurring, not because you seeking the outcome but because you aware of what you doing in the moment with regard to that intent. Do you see? Does it make sense?

For example, our intent is to give to you information that you can be placing into the book. Is this not so? Is it so?

Mmm.

No it is not.

(Laughing). It was to get Tony and me! I nearly said that there was a hidden agenda. No, no, no.

Think about what you did. You interpreted a statement we making.

Yes.

We not giving you information to put into the book because you not doing the book. Who is getting the information? We are not. We already got it.

Helen and then out there?

That is so. The information is being reflected off you two for this channel to hear, to put into the book for the world. Do you see?

Yes.

196

So, you are part of the outcome and the intent. As a consequence of the benefit your presence is giving for the channel to be having the information, you are being touched by the information you are hearing and it is having a impact upon your consciousness. So our intent is actually for our message to be presented through this channel into the world.

Fortunately for you, you part of the intent as a kind of a mutual admiration society. You going to get the benefit. You going to get the crankiness. No matter. You going to be touched by the consciousness of the energy being presented. Because our intent is clear of what it is we wish to do, the energy flows. Now, supposing we had been unclear in our intent. We will use your example, thank you very much. Supposing we were saying our intent is presenting information to these two individuals so it can be prepared in a book form. Well, you know, we going to be disappointed, are we not? Because you not intending to do it because your understanding of the intent is that the channel going to do it. So what is going to happen?
It won't go anywhere.
Exactly the situation. So you can have a very good intent but if your intent lacks definition, not clarity, definition, well you going to have confusion. Do you see?
Yes.
So this is why intent is so very important. As an overview at this point we not talking about whether you have a good intent or a ill intent. We simply talking about intent. When you formulate an intent it is usually formulated because of an idea or a concept or a feeling. Is this not so?
Mmm.
Well, you know that is not true either. The thought, the idea or the feeling is the stage at a physical at which you become

aware of the need to have an intent.
Oh, OK.

An intent has already been formulated by the Essential Being transmitting the message to the soul, who then sends the impulse to the personality, "This could be good idea. Or how do you feel about this?" Do you see?
Yes.
If therefore your connection between the Essence of who you Be, the soul and your personality is clear and open, without judgment or criticism, you going to have a very focused, disciplined, detailed ability to have a intent.
If you got a conflict in the communication line between who you truly Be and the personality you occupying, well, you know, what is going to happen? You going to go crazy. You going to start a war. You going to do something you did not in the least intend to do or you going to say, "Oh, it's all too difficult. I got to go to sleep." Do you see?
Mmm.
That is why it is so very important, as a physical consciousness, to develop the communication between the personality and the Divine Spark of Being. The communication is always present. It is the level of your consciousness that determines how you interpret the intent. So the example we gave earlier shows how easy it is to know and yet not to have definition.
Mmm.
So you almost there.

Well, you know, we going to give you a kind of analogy. You know you got to jump from this side of a river to that side. You know approximately how wide it is. You have a understanding of this. You even feel you got a understanding about how deep it is. So you say to yourself, "I got to reach

there. It is approximately this kind of a energy needed to make this kind of a jumping." And your approximately is 4 of your inches or 2 of your centimetres short of being able to land on the other side. There is not a slope to the other side. It falls in a straight line. Where you going to go?
Down.
Into?
The water.
Exactly. You going to fall into the water. Now approximately you know this water very deep. However, this water could be lot of feet or lot of metres deep. Do you see? And very fast. So what occurs is that not only do you not land where you intend to land, the force of the energy of the water carries you along little way to some other position. You still landing on the other side because you grab hold of something and get out of the water onto the ground. However, you have not arrived at the point of your intention to arrive. You arrived somewhere else. Do you see?
Mmm.
Because, approximately this is how far it is, approximately this is how deep it is, is not sufficient definition. Intent requires detail, focus, discipline and analysis. Vision requires the ability to open up to every possibility. Intent requires the need to focus on the specific aspect of whatever it is you are doing. Do you see?
Mmm.
We still talking about intent as a general. We not even started to talk about specifics. Already you can see there's a lot about this particular subject, can you not?
Yes.

You have a intent. You going to be a spiritual light worker. Oh, we better change that to Light Being because you not a light worker. You know this is what you going to be because

that is your intent. "Now I going to be a Light Being."
"Very good! We can have a celebration. We got another one already on the team. Thank you for joining us. What you going to be as a Light Being?"
"Well. I do not know. I just know I want to be a Light Being."
"Very good. How do you feel you can accomplish this?"
"Well, I do not know. I just know I want to be a Light Being!"

What is happening?
It lacks definition.
Exactly the situation. And the reason there is a lack of definition is the individual does not understand what it is he or she wants to be.
Mmm.
Therefore without the understanding how can that one become anything to do with it because there no understanding of it?
Mmm.
Now, just supposing, rather than this you want to be a medical practitioner. Well, you see, that is more clear. You got to do this kind of a study. You got to do this kind of a practise. Then you can be this kind of a practitioner. Is very clear, very direct. Why is this not clear and direct with regard to being a Light Being?
It's too general a statement, too broad a statement.
Which is the bigger picture.
Yes. I'd say it's like vision. It's out that way.

Exactly, so how you going to convert the vision into a reality? Where is the university you can be going to to be studying to be a Light Being?
Our Divine Spark?
The Divine spark.
The Universe? In meditation. Meditation is the university.

200

The Divine spark is your university, holds all of your wisdom. Through meditation is how you clear the dimensions to enable you to study with this one. Then you know whether you going to get your degree. However, what occurs?

What occurs... We have faulty lines? Or faulty connections!
What occurs is there is a lack of trust, belief or willingness to go internally.

Yes!
And so, the individual, who does not exactly understand what being a Light Being, or light worker means, because that is where they call themselves Light workers, then has to go asking every other individual, who appears to be already a Light worker. "Well. You know, I wish to be like you. How am I going to do it? Teach me."

Mmm.

So there is your butterfly kind of a energy because they going to one then another, then another. That is beautiful! They each gathering a little bit of further information or energy. As a consequence of the interaction, the one they going to or the group they going to is also having a benefit. That is appropriate. However, because the intent is cloudy, what occurs is that there is always a reason, there is always a justification, or an excuse to trust at an outer level than at an inner. The greatest reason is because "if I give to you my trust and it goes wrong, is your fault."

Mmm. Yes.
"If I follow you and your teachings and then I feel that you are using who I Be; or abusing the power I have chosen to give you because I following you, it is your fault. You are not spiritual. I am a victim." Do you see?

Mmm.

Is very clever, is it not? So, what you look at in such a

situation is what was the intent of the individual seeking to learn? The intent of the individual seeking to learn who sees themselves as a victim, is to prove that no matter what they do they are always going to be victimised because they believe they are not good enough.

Yes. Mmm.

If you believe your connection is not strong it is because you believe you are not good enough to have a strong connection: not because you doing anything wrong but because your own Divine Spark does not wish to be talking to you because you not a nice person. Do you see? Is very clever, is it not?

Mmm.

You choose to be a Light worker. We will stay with this phrase even though we have already expressed its inaccuracy. You choosing to be a Light worker. The first and most important step to take is to define your intent. You might assume that if you choosing to be a Light worker your intention is you want to do good. Well, you know, that is not always the situation. Of course, you want to do good but sometimes there are a lot of conditions placed upon how you want to do it: or what you require from your guidance in order to be effective. Do you see?

Mmm.

You got to look at your intent. Is your intent pure? Is your intent clear?

Are you being a Light worker because you believe more Light is needed upon your planet to assist it and its people in their evolution?

Are you being a Light worker because you have a genuine love and compassion for your fellow man and whatever you can do to assist them you are prepared to do? We not talking about being a victim. We talking about totally being committed to service.

Or are you talking about being a Light worker in the time that you have available to you when you not being busy doing everything you got to do because you physical?

Are you being a Light worker when you have your meditation transmitting healing to your planet? The remainder of your time got nothing to do with being a Light worker because, again, you in a physical body.

All of these are being a Light worker. All of these are beneficial.

However, the depth and the effect of your Light work is defined by the degree of your understanding and commitment. To your understanding, not to the ideal. Do you see?

And then you see, you see a Light worker quietly going about their business doing what they got to do. And here is another Light worker doing a lot of working in a very short intense period of time. Another individual comes along looking to see how to be a Light worker.

"Oh well, this one now doing very great amount, really intense. Must be very difficult. Where this one does not seem to having the same kind of a energy, quietly going about it. Must be easy."

What has occurred?

Well, they've misinterpreted. They've interpreted. They don't fully understand where or what's going on.

That is so. They have stood in judgment. This is going to be difficult. This is going to be easy. So the intent of what they are searching for has been defined by whether is going to be good or easy or difficult. So therefore already the intent

has a condition, based upon a perception.
Mmm.
Now we already been talking about that. We got to go back and work through all of this energy again. The moment you create an event, the first step of definition is to recognise and understand the beliefs you hold about it. Do you see?
Yes.
For example, you are choosing to be a medical practitioner. In choosing to be a medical practitioner there will be inherent within you beliefs about this kind of a work. There will also be judgments about it, based on experience or perception. If you do not recognise what are those beliefs and judgments, attitudes, you cannot go beyond them into an understanding that even with all of these beliefs and attitudes this is still what you feel you need to do from the heart of your Being.
If you never step beyond the understanding of the belief, then what you do is mechanical. Do you see?
Yes.

You are operating from your conscious mind and not from the heart of your Being. You are accepting that this is what you want to be without understanding why. You will be it and you may be very good at it but a vital ingredient is lacking. In your intent to be it, you have failed to recognise that it is part of a deep-seated need. And so then it becomes a mental exercise. Do you understand?
Mmm.
So, in defining the intent it is important to understand the beliefs you hold about it. It is then important to recognise the perceptions that you and others may have about what it is you are doing. Now, if at that point, you are feeling that you are in alignment with what is your intent, you are not going to be interested in the perceptions of others who may

disagree. Is this appropriate or inappropriate?
I would think it is inappropriate.
Why? Why is it inappropriate?

I feel that even though you know what you're doing is the right thing for you to be doing, on some deep level you are 100% convinced that this is right for you, I still feel that it's good to hear other opinions, other comments. It's good to be open enough to be able to listen to other people's viewpoints. You don't have to accept them and take them on board. I think it's good to be open because people see things differently.

That is exactly the situation. At the point where you have this kind of a intent, you have moved through your own belief into an understanding of where you be. It is not finished. You are still clarifying, defining your intent. You feel very comfortable about it. Unless you are open, you are quite accurate in your terminology, to the perceptions of other people, then it is possible to become closed to the total potential of what it is that is your intent. Do you see? It does not mean you got to accept the perceptions of other people. However, by listening to their perceptions, you are having another opportunity to recognise whether a perception expressed by another is enabling you to recognise within yourself a belief that had not as yet come to the surface.

So perception is a good means to see how clear your understanding of your belief of your intent is. Do you see?
Yes.
Listen to the perception and, as we have already discussed, you do not say, "Thank you very much. That is your perception. Goodbye." You say, "Thank you very much. I can see your perception. I going to go away and I going to feel

whether it is appropriate to my intent; whether there is something significant about it that may assist me in defining more clearly or whether it has no relevance in this particular instance. I will share that with you." Sometimes the perception of another has nothing to do with you and everything to do with their judgment of who they Be.

However, if you refuse to listen to what is expressed and to take it within you to test its ring of truth for yourself and your own intent, you are being closed. You are being conditional. What you are saying is, "I know I am being totally accurate. There is nothing I can learn from it." Do you see? What you are doing is you are denying the validity of the perception of another. Whether that perception relates to them or to you is irrelevant. That perception is real to that individual and therefore requires the honouring of its expression. Else you are simply closing down that individual, dismissing who they Be and their perception, which then creates another intent. Then that other individual got to prove to you and you got conflict of intents. Wasting of energy.

You come to your understanding. You get a perception about yourself or someone else very kindly offers one to you. It is a means for you of being certain of the foundation you are creating with your intent. At this point, when the perceptions of others are offered to you, is when you begin to define whether your intent is truly for good or ill.

It is not defined at the moment you arrive at that intent. It is defined for you by the perceptions of others. It is that which gives you the opportunity to test at the heart of your Being your reason, your need which gave rise to the intent. It is only through the expression of the perception of another that you will question the integrity of what you are doing.

This is why, when another offers a perception to you, if you dismiss it you are not standing in the integrity of your Being; you are not standing in the integrity of your intent; and you are not honouring the integrity of the other. Do you see?
Mmm.

It is at that point that you have the opportunity to claim for yourself exactly what you doing and more importantly why. Even if your intent is for evil, in the final analysis, it is simply an experience you are choosing as part of the overall pattern of your soul evolution.

There are degrees of intent.
"I am going to do this tomorrow because between now and tomorrow I might understand how I can do it."Or "between now and tomorrow someone else might do it for me."
Or "between now and tomorrow I might have a different concept, leading to a different intent, so I giving to myself plenty of space and time before I got to fulfil this intent."
What are you doing?
Waiting. Procrastinating.
Exactly, you are procrastinating. Why are you procrastinating?
Because you're not certain? You're not quite understanding?
Of?
What it is you really want to do. What you said earlier.
Not at all. It is because you are not certain **if** you want to do it. Do you see?
Yes.
Is not that you not certain of what you going to do. It's because you not certain of if you want to do it, any of it. You still not at the point of commitment. You still exploring, do you see? So it's not that it is an error. It is a degree. The intent has not been truly connected.

Mmm. That's what I was going to say.

Or it's that they don't fully see their intent to make that commitment?
They not certain if they want to **have** an intent.
Oh. Yes. A lot of the time could it be fear, perhaps?
We come to that. You are quite right, both of you. What you saying are aspects of intent. However, first of all, the weakest kind of a intent is the one which comes from having a lack of commitment to having an intention. We will clarify that.

Some people who either do not wish to be fixed in any place whether it be physically, emotionally, spiritually or mentally, or they wish to be free to be travelling about all over the place, exploring where they will. They will find it extremely difficult to make a commitment to have an intent that they want to follow through with.
Haven't they already got an intent not to stay committed?
Not at all. What they are saying is, "I just going to go where I will, when I will." That is their belief. You quite right. Underneath it the intent is to be free. However, in their consciousness, what they are saying is, "I do not intend to have any intention." What they will do is they will say that tomorrow they will do this and then they change it to prove to themselves that they still can.
Mmm.

It does not come from a fear. It comes from a need to prove that they are their own authority. They will be determined to have no intention because their reason will say that they are their own authority and don't have to be controlled or regulated. Therefore they don't need an intent. Whereas the truth of the situation is they do not believe they have the power to fulfil an intent. Do you understand?

Mmm.

Within them is a belief that if they say they going to do something, something will happen to prevent it occurring. So no point saying they going to do it even in themselves because they going to be disappointed, or they going to fail. For these ones what is more important is to help them to understand that their determination to have no intention has already been proven to be successful. Therefore they cannot fail with an intention because they already been living their life intending to have no intention and doing it very successfully. So you can assist these ones.

There are those who going to say, "Well, my intention is to be a Light worker. I do not know how to do it. So perhaps I better go study all about it first." Their intention is not to be a Light worker. Their intention is to study spirituality. However, in order to do so they got to have a good reason. By giving to themselves the outcome of 'by then I will be a Light worker' validates their intention to study.
Mmm.
It also serves another purpose. It gives them Time and Space in which to prepare themselves for the point at which they then got to be a Light worker: unless, of course, they suddenly arrive at a different intent, which validates the need to delay a little bit longer.

You got those who say, "I going to do this. This is my intent." And then they do nothing, or they appear to do nothing about it. Why do you consider this would be the case? Why do they have this intent and then they deliberately do nothing or they appear to deliberately do nothing to bring it into form?

Because they allow it to...they are open to what comes

with that intent. They're open to it. It's like a process? It's like they send it out? Is that where you're coming from?
Why do you think it does not occur or does not appear to occur?

I feel that when the person initially says, for whatever reason, that they've reached a decision, "I intend to do this task tomorrow." I feel that the initial statement of doing it comes from the spontaneity. It comes from a feeling of this is what they want to do. But somewhere between the point in time of making the decision and carrying out the task, they have come up with a reason not to do it. Basically they've given themselves a reason not to do it, whether that reason's based on fear or a quite good logical reason not to do it. The initial intention comes about from a feeling, a willingness to do it. Then suddenly some part of them kicks in or thinks no, comes up with consequences of what may happen, if they do this task. Then they change their mind.

Both of you are accurate. In certain situations when nothing is done or appears to be done, it is because the spontaneity of the moment has elapsed. If you take that to another level, it means the individual being spontaneous in that moment does not have a intention in true alignment with the integrity of Being. It is not an intention. It is a desire or an idea. Do you see the difference?
It is a desire or an idea to do this.
That is so. It is not an intention because if the intent was there in alignment with the integrity of the Being the intent would be fulfilled. So, at the point of that spontaneity, the intent, it is interpreted as an intent, the idea or the desire seems to be very suitable, kind of a joyful because spontaneity is usually from joy. "Oh, well, I going to do this." Do you see?

When the energy of that spontaneity dissipates, the intent cannot be fulfilled because the intent is not totally in alignment with the integrity of the Being. One of two things is required. Either the intent is released or the individual works upon aligning the two so the intent can be fulfilled. Do you see?

In order to do that you got to go back to the beliefs, the understanding, the perception and then you move forward again.

Now the one who appears to be doing nothing or is doing nothing, because they are putting their energy out, waiting to see what is occurring, has not fulfilled the first three stages. Why do we say this?

Because it lacks definition.

Exactly. Because until the intent is defined, what you putting out to see what will happen is a cloudy picture.

Mmm. I thought you meant that it looked like they'd set an intent and then put it out there and doing nothing. Or it looks like they're doing nothing.

Now we did not say anything about putting out. We simply said someone has an intent and does nothing or appears to do nothing.

OK. Yes, yes. My misunderstanding.

So, when they doing nothing or appear to be doing nothing, what they have done is to say to the Universe, "This is what I intend to do. Show me how to do it." And it is not happening. Do you know why?

It's not clearly defined?

Exactly.

We just give to you the answer because you already give it. By definition, what you saying to the Universe, for example is, "I wish to be travelling to the Moon." So the Universe in your sleep takes you for a little visit to the Moon. However, you did not ask to remember it and you did not define how you wish to get there. So you had your visit to the Moon but you did not remember that you did it in your sleep state. So, you going to say the Universe failed you. Your intent was that you wanted to go in one of your space rockets to enjoy the whole of the physical experience. Do you see? Definition is always important. If you are clear in your definition of what is your intent, then you can allow the details of how it comes to you to be resolved by your guidance and by your Divine Spark of Being.

So, for example, you wish to go to the Moon in a rocket. You wish to enjoy the experience. What occurs is the Universe creates a chance encounter. You talking to this fellow about wouldn't it be nice to be going to the Moon in a rocket. It is a dream that you always had but unfortunately you do not see any means of making it possible. What a coincidence! The fellow that you happen to be talking to has the means to make it possible for you. So you create your intent and its detail. How that intent then comes to you for you to manifest it, you leave alone. Do you see?

Mmm.

There are those who have an intent and they operate upon that intent. What occurs is they achieve it. Then they got no intent because they achieved what was the original intent, until they create another. Those who have an intent and achieve it, have achieved it because they have believed in the intent. They have understood its importance to them. They have perceived a way of achieving it and then they have allowed Time and Space to assist them in creating the reality. That is manifestation. When the intent is achieved there must be a period of no intent to allow the energy to then disperse. Is another cycle of creation and decay.

Mmm. It would then be open to exploration to start to find out what their intent is. What you said earlier, so that they can understand who they are, so that the new intent can be heard. No?
Please to clarify.

You were saying so one can decay but if there's that letting go of the old and bringing in the new, at the same time that Time and Space is being made or if they're in it, because they no longer have an intent, from the Divine Spark. You're saying that, would it be the exploration of them then waiting for them to hear what the next intent is or what their intent, belief, perception is.

It would be wonderful if it occurred consecutively. What happens is that at the point the intent is achieved, the Divine Spark is already saying to the individual, "You done it. What you going to do now?" Otherwise the individual would not feel the intent had been achieved, would feel they were still working upon that initial intent. So, that is when the Divine Spark first gives the notice to the individual, do you see?
Yes.
Not after the individual knows it's finished. That is what then creates the flow of energy for the individual to have a look at what was intended and to recognise its completion. Then there is the allowing of the fading away of the energy. In that period of letting go, the individual holds the knowing that there will be another intent. However, in that period, it is important that individual does not seek to set what could be the new intent. There must only be the holding of the knowing, not the exploring of the possibility of the new. Until the old energy has totally gone, that old energy can impact

upon the new intent. It can condition it. So what you're saying, that stage of the process, first of all the Divine Spark comes in to show this has been done. Then the individual begins to release that intent, knowing there got to be something else but not knowing what it is and not exploring it.

No, no. Not exploring the intent but it's that stage of Time and Space they are exploring a new belief. They're finding new beliefs.
No, no, no, no. Because you have not let go of the old. If you explore a new belief before you let go of the old, the old will limit the new.

Yes, I understand that but they are going to hit a belief about themselves as they're letting it go or see a condition.
Not at all. That is a stage later. As they let go of the old, all they are doing is releasing and allowing. There is no recognition. It is not a stage of recognition. It is a stage of letting go and allowing themselves to be in that stage of letting go. So that is the only energy being held. As that departs then what occurs is the re-evaluation. "This is finished. Who am I now? What do I believe about myself? What do I feel or see or think or perceive to be the next stage of my journey?" At that point, any belief you have accepted, any attitude you have claimed as a consequence of the old intent can then come to the surface without the energy of the old influencing it, because it's gone. If you explore that process in the period of releasing, you are going to create confusion.
No, no, no. I didn't mean it. It's a process.

You cannot evaluate whilst you are letting go, which is why it is important to define. Because many people in the process of letting go have a self-examination. Spiritually, they assess

214

where they are in the process of letting go. The moment you assess where you are in the process of letting go, the process stops because you are thinking about it, rather than allowing the energy to leave.

So if someone has a common answer, common comment, someone has a flu, diarrhoea, an upset stomach and they vomit, the common comment is, "I am letting go. I am releasing." Or from an outside person, "You're clearing. You're obviously releasing something." Invariably within the next two seconds the next question is, "What are you getting rid of? What is it you're clearing?" So, what you're saying is as soon as you focus on, "Why is this happening to me? What am I getting rid of?" you stop the process of clearing.
That is so.
However, whatever method you've chosen to clear it, whatever it is, I hope it doesn't happen but if I go home lunchtime and I start vomiting and someone comes up to me and asks, "What are you getting rid of? What are you releasing?" My answer to that would be that I'll work it out when I've finished.

Your answer is, "I do not yet know. The process is not yet completed."
Exactly. Yes.
So, therefore, to use your analogy, you are having this vomiting. If you say to yourself, "Oh dear, this is not a very pleasant situation. I wonder what it is I am trying to get rid of?" The focus, and the intent, of your energy has been diverted from releasing to thinking, to analysing. You do not analyse. You do not seek the answer until you finished with your vomiting. Only when you are empty, in this case literally, do you have created within you the Space and the Time to understand exactly what you released. Until it is all gone

you are only having some of the information and knowing, you not got all of it.

When you say to someone who got some kind of a problem, "Oh well, what is it you are trying to do?" (And in this case, we talking about physical not emotional, emotional is different) "What is it you trying to do? Why have you created that?" First of all, whether you intend to consciously or not, you are setting a stop in their process.

You may intend to be of assistance. However, you do not know what belief that individual is holding about that condition or about having that condition.

Mmm.

So by asking, "What are you trying to do? Why are you creating this?" that comment, with your intention of being helpful, can be perceived by the other as a criticism of who they Be and the process they are undergoing; depending upon how that individual is feeling within themselves. At such a time, when someone is having such a situation, you say to him or her, "I can see that you are in a process." (You do not define it.) "I hope your process moves forward in Light and Love." Nothing more. If they say to you that they do not understand what it means then you return to what we were saying earlier in another discussion. "When you have completed the process, please come to talk to me. We can explore together what it could be."

You do not give them the answer when they are in the middle of it because your intent to be of assistance actually creates an inhibition of their process.

Mmm. OK.

Their process, the intent of that process is to release the energy. They got to be empty before they can take into their consciousness anything else, which is what we were saying.

216

You got to let go with allowing because in the letting go with allowing you are not creating any belief or judgment that you later got to clear by another kind of a clearing, do you see?

In this instance, you can use this to release old beliefs and attitudes without taking on new, coloured by the past, because you let go of the past before you then explore the new understandings and beliefs you have about who you Be. And that is the true intent of being a Light Being.

Can I interrupt you here?
Please to do so?
Will this chapter go much longer time wise today?
Why are you asking?
Because there is about quarter of an hour before the channel's appointment arrives and I'm sure she'd like to have a cup of tea.
Very good suggestion. So what you are saying is to please define our intent because there is already another intent that has been set for the timing of this period. So you are defining and clarifying an intent. What we will say to you is that we will complete this discussion. We got to have another session, which is the final of our talking about everything. However, there will be one more, which will be your questioning about everything. That is when you have your turn to have discussion of us.

How many other people can we bring into this question time? Because I expressed to the channel that when I'm doing these sessions, listening to you dictating the book, I can only ask questions based on my perception. It's much more beneficial when Sherrie is there because she asks questions from her perception, which is different to mine.

That would apply to third, fourth etc persons. How many people can we pull into this question time? I have the number 6 but you may only agree to Sherrie and I.

Not at all. If you allow others to join what you are doing, then the balance of the energy, the number you incorporate, can only be maximum of three.
Us two plus one other?
Three others because then altogether with our energy you got six, which is the energy that we are trying to share with you.
Six or seven?
You got six. You got three others, you two and us.
And what about the energy of the channel?
Well, we not counting her, She not here. We using it. You only got six. She is not using her energy in her own right when we speaking through her, do you see?
Mmm.
So that is why is only six. We ask that there is the opportunity for this to occur within the coming week of your time, which means that you got to be very speedy about it.
Do we have to have the final chapter first?
That is so.

The final chapter has to happen within the next 7 days?
Most definitely and in that period would be good idea to be allowing those you are choosing to invite to be reading what already been offered so they can be pondering if they wish to be part of such a energy and what they wish to be asking about it, do you see?
Mmm.
Is this clear? Are you both awake now?
Yes.
Very good because in our last session both of you having

difficulty because of the energy. It always occurs when we talking about Karma you know. You always want to fall asleep because it's very heavy subject, do you see?

Yes. It depends on the intent.

Exactly the situation. It also depends upon what the perception is. So we thank you very much for your willingness to be part of this. You do not have to worry because we going to leave you.

Go with our blessing and our love until we meet again.

For I am John

Notes.

Notes.

Chapter Ten
Will to Good

And we bid you welcome. So you been having a interesting time of it, have you not?

Yes.

So have you.

Mmm.

Interesting that both of you were involved in the situation, not this channel. Do you see why? Both of you are going through the material together. Each of you therefore is able to give a perspective from one side or the other.

Yes, I've done that.

Do you see? So therefore you are a good example of what occurs when the energy is activated. Thank you very much.

You're welcome.

For those who are reading this particular chapter of the book, we just encapsulate, without going into any detail about it, that as a consequence of what has already been transmitted by ourselves one of the individuals accessed and lived through the whole situation we are talking about.

Yes.

The other individual was a means of observing, detaching, waiting and offering.

Yes.

Very good kind of a energy, don't you see?

Yes.

No. Not doing it again.

Very good! You can choose not to do so.

Been there, done that.

However, it does not alter the fact that both of you lived the energy. As a consequence, you come to a new belief, which you now got to work on the process of as you wish.

Mmm.

Or, to be more exact, as you will. That is intent, Will. So that is what we got to be talking about now. Every time you come to the point where you moved through a belief, you gone through the whole situation, let go, come to a new intent is because your Will has learned what it needed to learn in the experience. It is ready to move on.

The Will formulates the intent. It does not come from the mind. It does not come from the heart. As we were indicating in a earlier situation, they are the final stages in the creative, concrete form. However, the Will is the creative principle. It is the Divine Spark of your Being. So it is your Divine Spark, which formulates your intent.

The intent is then transmitted to the soul as a impulse. Think about it – an im-pulse because your Divine Spark is pulsating with the energy of the intent, sending it to your soul. Your soul is receiving it as a impulse.

Mmm. Yes.

Well, if you wish to be truly clever, you can say impulse is an abbreviation of the I Am pulse.

Ah, yes, very good!

So, the soul has the impulse about the energy. In your world impulse is translated as something without thought. That is exactly so because it has come from the Will.

So, is that why you feel driven?

That is a slightly different, more intense aspect of it. When you driven you feel as though you got no equality in the energy. You feel as though you being pushed. The soul is stronger than the personality at that point.

When you are in Divine intent then it is the impulse. The soul then begins gradually to be talking to the personality, trying to obtain its attention, transmitting thoughts of, "I wonder what it would be like to be doing this." Do you see? So that impulse that the soul receives is the Divine Will, your Divine Will, not God, we make this clear, having formulated an intent: the intent being to experience the nature for learning, transmitted to the soul.

The soul says, "Oh this is a very good idea. However, I done this before in another lifetime, not so very happy. " Do you see?

Yes.

So the soul at that point begins to interpret the impulse according to the blueprint of the current lifetime with regard to lessons learned and to be learned as a consequence of Karma. So, do you see, you have the whole energy?

Yes.

Now, at that point, you got to stop for a moment. You got your intent, which is interpreted by the soul according to Karma. It then takes on a colouration. You actually coming backwards through the process we been describing. For the Essence to make its intent known in the world, you got to go from the Essence, the intent, through the Karma, through the colour, through the sound because the soul sounds the note to enliven the energy of the personality physical matter so that the energy can be operating.

At that point the personality's attention has been captured. It begins to think about the impulse that the soul is transmitting. At that point the personality thinks it's very clever because it's got a good idea. Then it has to feel. The idea is a perception of the impulse. Then it got to feel how the perception feels. Finally, "This is creating this belief. I got to go do it." It is very clever, is it not? Do you understand?

Mmm. Very. Yes.

Makes it very simple.

In a way. (Laughs).

The difficulty arises when the personality sees the intent as a punishment, not a gift. The moment you begin to work with an intent, you going to access your Karma. We already talked about it. You going to access the beneficial and the not so good. The beneficial is taken for granted. While ever you accessing everything flowing very well you do not stop and say this is because you got good Karma. What you say is, "This is because Spirit thinks it's a good idea." Well, of course, because it came from Spirit.

There is no recognition that when it is flowing happily it is because of your own Karma assisting you. The only time Karma is talked about is when you got a problem. "Oh well, there is your Karma."

Yes, that's true.

Therefore Karma is seen as a punishment and it is not. It is neither one nor the other. It is simply a record of everything you have been and done which may assist or hinder anything else you going to do. Do you see?

Yes.

Very clever kind of a situation is it not?

Mmm.

Of course what occurs is that you say in your world, "Well, this is not working. Why is God punishing me?" "This is not working. What am I doing wrong?" "This is not working. Why does Spirit not assist me?"

It's an illusion.

It's a wonderful illusion. The reality is, "This is not working. Why have I created this situation for my learning?"

However, as we were indicating in our past situation, you got to understand how you feel because then you will see the belief. You cannot have understanding until you access the belief that is creating the situation. Always you got cycles within cycles within cycles; from the larger to the smaller; from the smaller to the larger.

To feel that you are a victim of your circumstances is to say that your Divine Essence has no intent or Will to Good for you. In fact, what you saying is that your Divine Essence got no Will; or if it does it only wishes or wills you to suffer. Well, you know, for it to be Divine must be unconditionally loving. If it's unconditionally loving, why is it going to punish you? Do you see? There is a lack of logic even to the reasoning, simply because there is no logic in such a situation. There is only emotion. When you got a lot of emotion, your thinking goes for a holiday somewhere.
Yes. Mmm.
Does this clarify this aspect for both of you?
Yes.
You got any question about it?
Not yet. Not at this point.
So, if it's so very simple, why is it your world is not living in peace and harmony?

Because they haven't accepted?
Well, I want to go to that they have attached to teachings and all those sorts of things and they haven't understood the principle of that; the acceptance of the Divine Spark and what it really means.
That is so. They have forgotten about their Being.
Yes.
Comes back to the beginning of this discussion.
We talking about a belief system and how what grows around the belief system is the interpretation. The Essence of the belief becomes hidden. Therefore anything that belief teaches, teaches the individual to hide from the Essence of their Being. Is not a concrete intent. The focus is so much upon the doing of the philosophy, the creed, the belief that the Essence of it is forgotten. Which is why we always saying to people, "You do not have to learn to be spiritual. You

already are. You simply have to remember who you Be. In remembering your Being, the doing flows into its natural order and place within the whole." Whereas if you focus on the doing there is no room for the Being.

Yes.

So, even in the evolution of your planet, you are at the point that because of your belief systems of the whole, the individuals are losing themselves, are confusing themselves, or they are finding themselves. The cycle is operating on all levels of Being. You got a very material reality. Everybody is acknowledging this situation. There are those who say materiality is non-spiritual; those who say that materiality is part of spirituality. Of course it is because it like the soul and the personality. You got to have your material reality because that is the personality that your world is wearing at a given point in time.

The belief systems are the soul energy, the spirituality, operating within it trying to find expression. If at a soul level you are trapped in your belief without understanding, you have fanaticism. If you have a belief that provides a understanding, you have a open minded energy. If you see the perception within the belief, then you begin to step into the recognition that it is the Essential Being, not the belief, that brings life. So the belief is simply another vehicle for the soul to explore and experience. Not simply your individual soul but the energy of your planet.

Mmm.

If you consider, many eons of your time ago, people very, very spiritual. Had not a lot of your technology. Indeed, had none of your technology. They had practical tools; were not able to communicate very well; dashing about the place trying to have some kind of existence, with great creatures

looming at different points eating them to pieces. Is that more beneficial than the situation you got now?
No.
All your people have done is that they have changed the physical live creatures to concrete creatures. Your institutions are your dinosaurs. Your buildings are your dinosaurs. So you still running away from them and do not know how because you forgotten that you are spiritual Being. At the moment of crisis, instinctively you seek to do and become stuck because you do not know what to do. You do not know what to do because you do not know at that point who you are Being because you got a judgment about it. Does this make sense?
Mmm. Yes.
Always you got the larger and the smaller, no separation between them.

Now, your Divine Will is a Spark of God. It is the creative power of your Being. It is your Being. You are being Divine Will. However, to be Divine Will means nothing. Do you know your Being of Divine Will? Are you able to talk to this Being, say, "Are you having a nice day?"
I could but I'm not allowing it.
Exactly the situation! That is because your Divine Will has a purpose for you, an intent. That intent is for you to be Love in Action. Very Good! So, the Divine Will formulates the intent of being Love in Action. Then the Akashic records come to the fore.
"Oh, well, in this particular situation, this individual was being Love in Action, ended up slaughtering 20,000 people. In this situation, this individual was being Love in Action ended up being torn to pieces for saying something inappropriate."
Just two such situations. There is a Karma, not a punishment. A Karma that comes from the belief that Love

in Action is painful. Everybody on your planet must meet this belief at some point.

So, there is the Karma. The impulse transmitted to the soul, the colouration, is to be Love in Action. According to the previous experiences you will have had in other lifetimes, you will interpret, at a soul level, what Love in Action means. So already you moving slightly away from the pure intent. Is like the jumping across the river, do you recall, when you approximately know it? But you end up little bit further away. *Mmm.*

You approximately know it because the soul has interpreted it based upon the unredeemed energy within itself that it is seeking to heal. Do you see?

Mmm.

So the soul says that you got to go into the world, be Love in Action. Now, in order to do this, we need a personality that is going to be born in circumstances whereby at some point we can activate the Will to Good. That is the second divergence. Because Love in Action has been interpreted, the Will to Good will be interpreted according to how Love in Action is perceived.

Here is your perception.

If you believe that because your intent is good, and you know better because you now active alive spiritual Being being on a path of Will to Good, you may burn somebody at the stake in order to save their eternal soul. Well, where is the Will to Good? What you done through your determination on Will to Good, you given to this soul the belief that in order to express who they Be they going to have to suffer. The interpretation of the initial impulse leads to a misperception of how the energy is to be carried forth into your world.

Therefore the moment you begin to be Love in Action, to develop the Will to Good, the first things which occur are situations which cause you to have another look, both at your perception of it and your interpretation of it. Until you are totally aligned to the Divine Will, your own Essence, you always going to approximate. You not going to eventuate. So your people become frustrated because 'I doing all of this.' 'I being very sincere.' And they are. However, they missed the point that if it is not working, the intent cannot be totally aligned. Therefore have a look at where there has been a interpretation or a misperception.

It does not mean that what they are doing is wrong! What they are doing is right because in the doing it enables them to create the opportunity for clarity. Then they have another look. "Oh well, I was seeing Will to Good as having to burn these individuals. Now I am seeing that perhaps there is another way whereby these ones can receive the message and live to fulfil it for themselves, rather than having to die to do so." Changes the concept altogether because if you want them to live to fulfil it, you cannot burn them. You got to find another way to change their perception or to plant seeds within them. Is this clear?
Yes.
Is why we are saying to you again and again, do not seek to convert another. Share: do not, however, say to another, "Your belief is totally wrong" and prove it. When you take away that individual's belief before they are ready to release it, you taking away that aspect of their Being, which sustains their will.
Yes.
When the belief is invalidated, the Will to Good is nullified. Therefore the Love in Action has been demonstrated as conditional love, rather than Universal love. The teachers

of your world, the Master Teachers, the Ascended Masters, the Brotherhood of Light, all of these are ones who have moved through this process. They have, whatever the trials and tribulations of their experience, ultimately returned to "What is my belief? What is my understanding? What is my perception?" as stepping-stones to moving beyond it.

It is in clarifying these areas that Karma is healed. As Karma is healed the soul energy is purified because that is what the soul is carrying. The beneficial Karma goes to the Essence of your Being and is used to help you. However, the soul contains the unredeemed Karma. So, yes, there is something beyond Karma, the Karma of the soul. There's the Karma of the Divine Spark of your Being because that is pure love, that Karma. It is everything that you have ever been and done from experience, empowering the Essence of your Being, to be Divine.

Only when all of that is redeemed do you have the true Resurrection. Then you got no soul. You do not need it. You are literally reborn fully as Love in Action in Personality, capital P. It is at that point that you have the Divine Will or intent to choose what is your service to God. Until you come to that point, everything you doing on this Earth plane is preparation, training and purification. You are still serving your God. However, in this place you are serving the Divine Essence of your Being, who is serving God. So you got another intermediary. Do you see?
Yes. Mmm.

It is only when you purified the soul energy, it is gone, you standing in the Personality, you then are asked, " What is the path of Love in Action, the Will to Good, you are choosing to follow now?" That is when your final choice is made. Do

you understand this?
Yes.

So, is very good, is it not? You got all of this focus upon the physical when in actuality it is a very small part of the whole? However, you see, what happens is that because you not trusting who you Be, because you forgotten who you Be, it is only the physical that you can focus on because it is the only thing that is certain. Do you see?
Yes.

You keep having the situations lifetime after lifetime, or within one lifetime, until suddenly you say, "Oh! What a wonderful situation. However, I do not need it." Recognition. At that point of recognition that energy pattern is broken. Then you have the allowing of the letting go; doing nothing with it, just letting it disperse, dissipate. Then away you go again, another intent.

Mmm. Can I ask then, because that's how I felt in my own process throughout this book, is that when I let go of that belief that I carried in my soul, I felt like I had nothing. I said to Tony that I feel helpless, powerless, like I've got nothing. Part of me can understand that you don't take away a belief because then there's no foundation. Another part of me was asking where my beliefs were, that I had and was strong with? Tony was saying that they were, and I was aware that they would be, what I've been learning or will become my new beliefs. So you are talking about getting to that point and letting go? Could we have an idea of what a person could do in that sort of situation so that they don't reattach or fall into 'I don't have a belief?' Because that is empty.
In our last interaction, that is exactly what we were discussing with you. There has to be a point of feeling empty. If, whilst you are in that point, you try to fill it you never

going to recognise clearly the belief you are building.

So that's in that......so it's belief as well that you are letting go?

You come to a point where you learn something. You have a realisation that a belief is no longer valid. Usually a belief is something that has been a integral part of your life. So, to recognise that it is invalid, is like losing a limb. A part of you is being taken away. Except that you are the one who is pulling off that limb. In a physical such situation your body would go into shock, would it not?

Yes.

Your brain would say, "This is too much of a situation. We got to close down on all systems in order to sustain life." And according to the individual's situation, life is sustained or released. Is the same when you losing a belief. What occurs is you taking away that limb so your personality goes into shock. It is like your body. "I lost this very important part of my Being." Your soul says, "Close down. Feel empty." Because the shock is an emptiness. At a physical level, when you are in shock there is a nothingness. That is the emptiness. There is a nothingness because you got nothing to which you can cling.

You got nothing to attach to and that is important. If you allow that emptiness, with the knowing that there will be a new intent or belief, you giving to yourself a kind of a lifeline, but you not trying to work out who you are now or how you are going to develop that belief. You are allowing the emptiness: as the shock naturally dissipates the body heals. As the emptiness gradually clears, the soul's communion with the personality becomes stronger and the intent can then be impulsed to the personality of formulating the new belief without any poison of attachment to the old.

Do you see?
Yes.

So, to return to what you saying, if you can allow yourself at that point of emptiness to say, "This is exactly perfect for my process." Rather than, "I feel empty now what am I going to do? Have I done something wrong to feel so empty?" your emptiness is going to disperse more quickly because you not fighting it, you flowing with it.

Would I be able to ask then, you said with that lifeline, is it my Monad, Divine Spark sending me the message "now you understand the power of love moves through you"?

That is so because that impulse, that lifeline cannot come through the soul because the soul interprets it. The Essence can give to you the feeling that there is more. And it is pure. You cannot attach to it because you do not know where to go with it because you need the soul to interpret it.
Yes. Makes sense.
However, this soul cannot do the interpretation until it's finished with that part of the healing. So your Essence is sustaining your creative Will simply to Be. And in this case to be empty, that is the creative aspect of it, the emptiness, until the soul finished letting go of that Karmic energy, sending up to the Essence the purified energy to make the Essence greater and then saying, "Thank you very much. We done that. What is next?" And away you go again. Do you see?
Mmm. Yes.
Does this now clarify what was occurring in our last interaction?
Yes.

Is why we were saying to you no, no, no because if you stay with the thought that you got to evaluate while you are letting go, you are in the tunnel. You come out of the tunnel into the light of day and then you say that looking at this tunnel it is a square shape, or a round shape. Or that there is this in it. That is the evaluation of the experience. It is very important. However, you got to get out of the tunnel first else it going to fall in on you. Then you got to go right back to the beginning of the whole situation. This is where you change the label of your belief not the belief itself.

So your Will, the power to be creative, is working very well in you because what you doing is you saying to it, "All I need from you is to give to me another label so I do not have to go to the heart of this belief and release it." Do you see? "I can still feel comfortable because I am saying to myself that I moved forward since it is now no longer this label. I am at this label." When in actuality it is the same energy again, and again, and again, life after life after life. Is very boring. You know, the ultimate point is, it is your soul that becomes bored with it.

Oh! Can I ask a question with that or is that for the question and answer time? There was a part with Time and you mentioning this. I got bored. I felt really... I had so much Time and so much Space because we stepped out of Time. I was absolutely bored. People are saying they are so bored.

Of course! They have at that point come to the point when they slowly saying, "When are you going to awaken to the fact that you do not wish to be doing this anymore?" What happens is that the personality says, "This is a very frightening kind of a situation though because if I going into this belief and I release it, there is the fear of the emptiness."

234

OK. We don't want to go beyond boredom because we'll go to the emptiness.
And the emptiness is frightening. What if you go into the emptiness and you never come out of it? The emptiness is a black hole, do you see?
Mmm. Yes
Of course you never come out of it. Think about it!
You've been reborn.
Exactly the situation. The you that goes into it is not the you that comes out of it. That is another kind of a resurrection, do you see? So you having this energy opportunity open to you all of your time. It is your belief, your perception, your understanding, in other words your attachment to third dimensional reality, which inhibits you from moving into fourth.

When you change your belief, you are stepping into fourth and fifth to do so. And then, because you had such a fright with the emptiness, you quickly scramble back to the third dimension to receive the next intent because it safe. Then you become bored again. You do not maintain your consciousness beyond the third. The moment you start to get a intent because it is a habit to be thinking, to be feeling, the soul says, "Now just a moment. You been having a very good time talking to that Essence. However, now you got to be working again." There is the doing. "This is how you got to do it." The soul interprets the impulse of the Divine Spark. So then you as the individual, say that you got to study, to ponder, go into a monastery, got to go fight a war as your expression of that impulse because that is the perception of it. Does this clarify for you?
Yes, it does for me. Did it help you in having to put up with me? (Talking about Sherrie's experience of the teaching.)
It doesn't explain why I put up with you.

Thank you, Tony. Yes. If you hadn't been like you were then, that emptiness would have....I can see that explosion was shock.

Shock and anger. "Why do I have to feel this? Why do I have to suffer? Why can it not be love and peaceful and beautiful?" Do you see?

It can. If you allow the letting go, it can be peaceful, beautiful and loving. If you attach to what you are releasing for fear there going to be nothing else, you got shock and horror, not shock and healing. Do you see?

And make no mistake, there going to come time when you going to do it for him.

Too easy!

It is always a mutual exchanging of the energy.

Too easy. I just hope I'm as good at it as he is!

Just be gentle with me.

You are very good at it. However, you do it different to this one. When it is his turn, you got to give him spiritual clip upon the ear.

I went like that – impulse.

Because he is of a gentle disposition, gentleness is not going to activate him.

Is that why gentleness activates me?

Exactly. Because he is of a gentle disposition, you got to tell him what to do because that angers him. Do you see? Not in sharing but in ordering. "Well, you got to do this." Or "why are you not doing this kind of a situation?" He get very cranky about it, do you see?

Yes, I have one at home too.

Exactly the situation. So, he become very cranky about it and then what he do is very clever. He then sets out to prove you are wrong. Well, you won because in proving you wrong, he actually do whatever his soul is telling him to be doing.

Oh, I've had that earlier in my life. Yes, I've done that too.
You did it for self value because you felt judged. He will do it, not because he feels judged, but to prove to you he knows what he is doing.
Oh yes, that's true.
So therefore in that situation, you actually succeeding. Is this not so?
I don't know. I turned the tape off. (Laughs)

However, is in your consciousness. Is this not so?
Yes, probably.
Indeed, if you told you cannot do something you want to know why. Then you try to work out if you can do it. Yes, you can so you going to do it – and you do!
Mmm.
That is your creative Will in operation. So, if you are sympathetic to him, he simply going to continue. He not going to do anything. Do you see?
Whereas if sympathetic to you, initially you take it. "Oh, thank you. You are understanding how I am feeling." Until you realise you do not want sympathy because you are not in sympathy with yourself.
Then you criticise yourself and the anger builds within you. You go round and around in your head because you are so sensitive, the safest way is to put it into your head. You go round and around and around until finally you got to explode. You got no more room!

Your head is so full you got no more room for anything so you got a volcano situation. Is fortunate if those about you are used to it because then they are simply just going to allow the volcanic matter to erupt and not attach to it, which is what this one did. Allowed you to explode, listened because you needed to feel you were being heard. If you recall you accessed through your tunnel that you do not listen to yourself. So he demonstrated that he was listening so that you could know that you were listening to what you were saying.

Yes. Yes.

In the process, you realised what was the conflict of your own belief system. He did not have to say a word to you. Well, few words to sort of encourage the process.

Yes, Tony then focused more on the affirming of a new belief.

Exactly, exactly. You had already been in the emptiness. This is why we say to you fear is such a powerful tool. When you got a individual in fear of anything, you are controlling and manipulating that individual.

Therefore, Love in Action in your world, the Will to Good, can best be utilised in assisting others to move through their fear because once they move through it they claim the power of their Being without any fear of their own ego.

Yes.

They know their ego is in alignment.

They've come home, yes.

So, bit of a longwinded answer to your question. However, does it clarify?

Yes.

Very good! Do you have a question?

Not at this point?

Is there anything you wish to know to do with the intent, with regard to the Essence of your Being and how it operates? Of necessity we been little bit narrow in the definition because we showing you how it connects to the subjects we been talking about as a process of evolution.

However, is there anything you feel it could be beneficial to be asking?

There could have been one thing earlier on. I might have to save it for question time. I can't remember. It's to do with intent, personality and Karma. I'll wait until I read this chapter.
Very good because then you will have an understanding of what it is you wish to be clarifying. Therefore we can be of assistance with a belief and the elucidation of it.
What we done is we encapsulated everything.

And I feel like I'm coming through my experience so I'd like to read it and then ask my questions.
I feel I have a desire to cross the river but because my intent isn't clearly defined I might end up downstream.

Then you will, because your feeling is telling you this is a potential.
Indeed.
If your feeling is telling you this is a potential, it is because within you in your belief, you have a aspect of it which is going to take you down the stream. So, when you have such a feeling, look at your belief and see where there is not necessarily a conflict but there may be a tension; lack of clarity in a belief itself.

Yes, that's what I was referring to about the question. I know there's a question but I haven't got it clearly in my head. When I read this last chapter I will understand what I am going to ask.

Listen to what we were saying. Look at the belief. When you read the chapter, a belief within you will be activated. Until you look at the belief being activated and understand

it, you will not have the exact clarity in the asking of your question.
Yes.
So that is why we say to you not to read about it or think about it. Read it and recognise the belief being activated, understand the belief, then think about how you can verbalise your question.
Oh, yes.

We are emphasising this because it is a process that is missed in your world. You know, there lot of beautiful souls on your planet who have a very strong connection to the Essence of their Being and no common sense. Common sense is when you are using your spirituality and your five physical senses in unison. What they do is, "I got this wonderful connection. I do not have to concern myself with the material." Well, as we have asked before, if that is the situation why are they in a physical body?

They are in a physical body because through their connection the Love in Action, the Will to Good of their Divine Essence, can show others how to make the same connection and utilise it in a practical manner in your world. Your healing circles are wonderful. Your circles of sounding, of transferring energy around your planet, are wonderful. However, if you do not, can not, will not share your own connection and how it occurred and developed with another, you are not lighting the path for anyone. What you are doing is you are leaving those others to stumble along in the darkness and you are clearing up the difficulties they are creating for themselves.
Do you see? Do you understand?
Mmm. Could I have another example? No, could I have an example, please?

Very well. You have, we give you very good example because this is something we been very stern about, the situation of the New York energy. So, you have this kind of atrocity situation. Many souls passing over, lot of healing sent to this place of New York; lot of messages of sympathy, gifts of understanding. Very beautiful energy.

However, the moment the decision was taken to be going to this other place and be bombing it and its people, where is the sympathy, where is the expression of healing? So, therefore your healing circles are conditional upon whether you perceive what is happening to be right or wrong. Take it a stage further. There are those souls sharing the wisdom of what occurred. So they saying this is part of a change of consciousness. In order to be more than simply sending out healing for what has happened, if these ones were to teach individuals how to take responsibility for their own process in a practical manner, there would not be the need for so much healing.

So, they could say to the ones they are sharing with, "We give to you a suggestion. War is not a good alternative. Please to be making contact with all of your government people, telling them you do not like it, to stop." It does not occur because another belief interferes. That belief is called patriotism. Patriotism is dangerous because it says 'my country, my people, have more value than yours.'
If you look at the number of people who died as a consequence of New York, you got about four and a half thousand souls: lot of souls, beautiful souls who performed a service. Then you look at this place of Afghanistan. How many thousand people are refugees? Have no home, no food; who are trying to survive.

Where is the balance? Where is the Love? Where is the justice? Where is the freedom and liberty to Be all you can be, which is what your United States of America was founded upon. Where is their compassion for the innocents in this place? There was plenty of compassion for the innocents of their place. Do you see? And, what will occur is, because that belief of patriotism is being fed, compassion is being deadened. So, here is your situation again, compassion for others is being deadened because these people are being told that the outcome is being justified by any means. Once you begin to follow that path human life counts for nothing. A soul's journey is unimportant because the outcome is more important than the individual soul.

So those who are teaching spirituality, who are sharing these beautiful messages of healing, need also to be saying," However, at a practical level, I am going to be doing this. Do you wish to join me?" Is no good to be anchoring energy upon your planet if you do not then use the energy in a concrete form to change consciousness. If you do not use it, all you are doing is being a saviour. And you know what happens to saviours. They got to be crucified because the people they are saving have not changed their perception, their belief, their understanding. There is going to come a point in time when the people they are saving are going to say, "You are a threat. You a crazy kind of individual. We got to do something about you." So, the very people you trying to save, going to terminate your existence. Do you see?
Mmm. Been there. Done that.
Indeed. So did we. We had a very important life. You may have heard of it. It was with this Master Teacher Jesus. We had the same kind of a situation. Well, you know, we not going to do that again. We learned from it. Does this answer your question?

242

Yes.

Is there anything else you feel we can be expressing to elucidate?

No. Not at this point in time.

Then we will say this as a extension of what we were saying.

Your United States had a opportunity to change your world consciousness. It did not. However, your United States is a symbol of every other country in your world that at any given moment has the same choice and chooses not to.

So, you cannot simply say that it is the fault of the United States of America because that is a judgment. The moment you do that you got to have separation because some are going to say yes and some are going to say no. You got a wonderful division. If you can understand why this country believes this is what it got to do and then point a different perspective to the belief, you are not creating a conflict. You are planting seeds because ultimately it is through this United States of America that the new consciousness will finally emerge.

Because it is such a material energy, it is only when its energy changes that the energy of your whole world can change.

Interesting that it's classed as the super power.

Of course! It is a super power. It is a super power, at the moment, of materiality and of conditional love. And it is going to be the super power of spirituality and unconditional love. It has a very important role to portray. However, at the moment it is just having a good time, playing war. That is what it is doing, playing war. "Well, I going to shoot you. You got to shoot me."

It's still creating people to break out of old beliefs.

That is so. It is serving a very valuable purpose. One of the things that will come out of this is that people will be reminded that as individuals they have a lot of power. At the moment they saying that they just one individual and got no power. They forgotten, for example, your war of Vietnam. It was the voice of the people, which created the ending. Do you see?

In the final analysis, it is always the voice of the people because (this is what you got to remember, is very sneaky!) your government people want you to like them and elect them again. Well if you saying, "We do not like you. You got to change it." They quickly going to do what you want so they can stay where they be. Very clever.

So, as far as we are concerned that actually sums up everything we been talking about. As you know one more chapter for the asking of the questions about anything the individuals already selected. Then time to be putting it all together and throwing it out into your world. Going to make a bit of a splash you know.

Yes.

We thank you for the opportunity to be creating this, for going through the experience, each of you in your different ways, so therefore you got the wisdom of the material.

As always go with our blessing and our love until we ready to start the next one! Do you see?

Yes. We might be down that river! (Laughs)

We very good at fishing! You forgot we were fishermen. Do you see?

So, therefore go with our love and our blessing until we meet again.

For I am John.

Notes.

Notes.

Chapter Eleven
Some Questions and Answers

Welcome. We just letting you know we here.

Welcome. Any questions about Chapter One?
My main question on chapter one is for more clarification on the Jesuit teachers.
What is it you are asking?
Who are they?
They were the teachers who were the training officers, if you will, within the Roman Catholic Church, as you call it. The Jesuits were an order within the Church. Their purpose was a kind of a focus upon the teachings. They were the law. Does this clarify for you?
Yes, thank you.
Lot more involved. However, that is a simple kind of a encapsulation of the whole situation.

I have a question. You talked about self-loyalty being important and that people will be judged as being self indulgent or self centred. You said that's a different kettle of fish. Could you give us an explanation of self indulgent and self centred?
Well, you got a lot of time? This is going to be a long one.
Perhaps a small one?
When you are self-centred you are focused upon your own Being without thought or care for the Beings of others, from a self-indulgent perspective. You so focused upon yourself and what you going through, you got no time, you got no energy, you got no thought for other people. Does this clarify?
Yes.

Any questions for chapter two?

Yes. I have noticed in chapter two that you have spoken about self-sacrifice. It has made me wonder because as a bomber pilot I was accused on three occasions of being a murderer. Now, what was I to do? Did I do the right thing? Or did I just sit back and allow what was going on, the rape and murder of all the countries in Europe and do nothing, play no part in that? I would like your opinion, please John?

Very good because this enables us also to clarify little bit about what we talking about in the final chapter of the book also, which is patriotism. With regard to the fighting within a war, what you are doing at that point of your time is that you are standing in the Light of who you Be and what it is you believe. So, therefore, to be your bomber kind of a pilot, you not doing the wrong thing. You are standing in the Light of your own beliefs, your own ideas.

However, what could have occurred, any other alternative, would have occurred earlier in the situation, before ever your war situation came to a point of fighting. That is the time, as it is building up, and your politicians talking about what they going to do, what they not going to do. Then you have the opportunity to try to avert a war; unless you got a situation such as this one with the Hitler because he was there for a world learning. Now, in that situation, there was nothing you could have done to prevent the war energy. In fighting, you were fighting for the Light. Yes, other people were dying on all sides of the situation. Is not a murderer. Those who gave their lives on both sides did so as part of the clearing of the energy. Does this answer for you?
Thank you.

Then we clarify just a little bit more. In the final chapter we talking about patriotism being dangerous because it is. From the situation, if you are very patriotic individual, without thought for what is occurring in your country, just for the pride of the country itself, then you can be very easily manipulated. You can be called upon to do things in the name of the country that under normal circumstances you would never even contemplate. So, patriotism, when it is unthinking, when it is purely 'my country above all others' and intolerance of all others, is where you can be manipulated.

And in such a situation, you are accountable because you not thinking about who you Be, what you doing. In your situation, a war situation, those who are fighting are fighting for a belief in fight, do you see? They are not held accountable unless they go beyond the parameters of that situation such as your atrocities, where someone has a power, uses that for mutilation, self gratification all these kinds of a thing. That is accountable but in the normal situation where you simply following the orders because you believe in the right of what you doing, no accountability, no murderer. Does this clarify?

Thank you very much, John.

You are very welcome. We thank you because it gave us opportunity just to expand little bit more about it. So, you got another question?

When you judge something or someone and it's a belief within you, to have this judgment, because after you've had this judgment comes the questioning and the recognising of the belief, then the understanding. Is this the way it is? That's how I've understood it. So if I judge somebody, and obviously my judgment is within a belief of my own, as soon as I've judged it then I've recognised it as my belief, then comes the understanding and the claiming of it being my belief?

For you, for those who are following their personal growth that is so. They have a judgment and if they are awake they recognise they made a judgment, and then they can look at the belief, look at the understanding, clarify.

However, for lot of people they live in judgement. This is why we say you got to go beyond judgment because while ever you live in judgment of a situation you never going to move forward. It is recognising that it is a judgment that enables you to change it, do you see? Does this clarify?
Yes, yes.

Very good! And those who do not, who end their life still with this kind of a judgment based on a belief, going to come back, have another go, do you see?
If you judge your judgment then you stifle your growth of seeing it and moving forward.
If you judge your judgment, you never going to admit you got any! The moment you admit you got a judgment you got to judge the judgment. Then you going round and around in your circles. You going crazy, do you see? Until you stop. It is not good to judge the judgment.
No, to see the judgment, I mean.
It is good to recognise the judgment.
Thank you.
You are very welcome. You got another question?

No, we'll move on to chapter three.
I have a question. I saw perception in a different light. Perception, anything to do with belief system. That's it.
What exactly are you saying? You made a statement without a clarification of your statement, do you see?

I've seen a perception of something. Is it always my belief that I've seen it in that way.

That is so. Even when it is a world belief, if you have accepted it, it has become your belief. So, perception is always, without exception, personal. Even if, for example, we were to say to you your Earth is round, you will recognise this particular situation, and everybody say the world is round and you agree with them, you agree because it is your perception. If you say that you disagree, it is not round at all, you are disagreeing because it is your perception. Makes no matter. Do you see?

Yes, thank you.

You very welcome. Anybody else got a question about perception?

No.

So therefore you all got your own perception and happy with it.

So we perceive.

Exactly the situation.

In chapter three we were talking about the group. I felt because I knew the group, I understood that bit of the chapter in the book. I wonder if people reading the book who don't know the group or the energy, is it going to confuse them?

Not at all because people are people are people. You going to get exactly the same situation as described wherever you living. Where one individual developing some kind of a theory and the other very busy, they still going to say, "Excuse me, what I doing is more important, more intense, more critical than you." So makes no matter about it.

We could have said this is a group in this place of Timbuktu, or Pluto, do you see?

Yes.

It makes no matter, the energy the same. Indeed, when it come to the point we probably going to make the suggestion you take out the specific area.

OK. So we talk about this overseas group in the book as a third party?

That is so. A group. Not a group and where it is.

No specifics of domicile or where it is.

That is so and you going to change the naming also. However, you not going to be changing your naming and your naming *(pointing to Tony and Sherrie)* because you two got no choice about it, do you see? That is our perception.

Sherrie's questioner 1 and I'm questioner 2.

That is your perception!

It's my belief, yes.

Very good!

Chapter three brought up questions for me but I feel it's for the end, the glossary. I don't have a question for three.

I have a little question for chapter four. I just would have liked to have known a little more about perfect time and perfect space.

Well you know, that is a whole new energy. All we doing in this particular situation of a book is to be planting seeds. People going to go away and say, "Well, I thought I understood that. However, perhaps I could have some more information about it." If we try to give you everything about everything within it, we never going to finish it.

Yes.

You got to wait for your perfect Time and your perfect Space in order to ask your question.

And it will be answered at the perfect Time and Space.

That is so.

252

OK. Chapter Five, any questions about this?

Yes, I have one. Perhaps this will go into another book or somewhere else but I'm very interested to learn of the creatures of great intelligence below the surface that we know in this planet. Is this the time or is it later that we can ask about them?

That is another situation also because, you know, is a whole story about these creatures. There are different kinds for different purposes. They been in that place longer than your man has been living in a physical form upon your planet. Their intelligence and their capability is such that they are able to operate in total darkness and yet be their own light source. Think about that for a situation. Is that not what you are all trying to become? They already done it! And when they finished, well, they going into Space literally. However, as we say, lot more information about that in another kind of a situation.

Thank you, John.

You are very welcome.

Still on that same topic, are those creatures in a physical form in the ocean? In the deep ocean, five or six miles deep?

Some are physical; some are non-physical. It depends on their purpose for Being. Do you see?

Yes.

Does this clarify for you? Very good, the energy becoming little bit discombobulated. Perhaps you better be breathing, do you see?

OK. That's chapter five; anything else for chapter five? Thoughts or comments?

Well, I've just got a comment of Space. I find that I've got to read it again.

That is good.

Yes. I simply got when I was reading it that Space is simply

Spirit.

That is so. It is consciousness. It is Spirit in consciousness. Spirit **is** consciousness. You cannot separate the two. So Space is consciousness, is Spirit. You know in your religions, you talk about your Holy Ghost, your Holy Spirit, or your Prana being Spirit. It is so. It is consciousness of All That Is. What you do with it determines what your journey is going to become. Do you see?

Mmm.

However, we would suggest you read again because there little bit more to it than that.

Oh yes. I realise that.

Lot of home working, do you see?

Yes.

Do you have another question?

Chapter six, anyone?

Yes. I have a few questions, John, on chapter six. When you speak or tell us of the speaking that takes place, it made me wonder if perhaps it was to do with the speaking in tongues? When Jesus was crucified and the disciples were assembled after his resurrection, there came the winds through the room and they spoke in tongues. We have certain religious people with us today who speak in tongues. I wondered if perhaps, whether this sound you speak of that comes from us, say from our soul, that was what you were referring to?

Not exactly the situation. Your sound is exactly that, a sound, kind of a note, do you see?

Yes.

When you speaking in tongues, you combining lot of sound, lot of notes, if you will, together to form a vocabulary. Whether you understanding the vocabulary or not is irrelevant. It is still a kind of a combining of notes, do you see? So that is like your music with your melody. The melody conveys a kind of a energy. The speaking in tongues convey a kind of a energy, a consciousness. The true sound is the one note that is who you Be. Do you see? Does this answer your question?

Yes. Thank you. I have another one. When you speak of the power of sound, I wonder whether perhaps this refers to the destruction of the walls of Jericho?
Of course! Sound in its own right, if you will, as a force, a energy is used for construction and destruction. You know, at the point where your own soul is no longer required, it is giving forth of the sound that shatters the energy of it. So that you are then one with your Divine Spark, your God. Do you see?
Yes, thank you, John.
You are very welcome.

I have another short question. With the modern music of today, I find it so very loud. To me, I find it almost sometimes reaches the stage of distressing, of where it distresses me. I can't in my own mind call this music. I wonder if there is something missing from me, or what it is? Perhaps you can help me, John?

It is not a lack within you. It is a recognition within you. This modern kind of a situation, you are quite accurate is not a music. It is a noise. It is a noise because the energy of these people creating it is confused. If they are confused within their own energy, they cannot create their own sound. So what they do, they try to put as much of these notes together, to form a energy in the hope that somewhere within it they find who they Be. It is distressing for you because you are sensitive to this energy, as are many in your world.

So for you is as though you are being beaten. Do you see?
Yes.
Well, you know, you just got to switch it off and send love to those who creating it, so they can find the heart of who they Be and then is all finished.
Thank you, John.
You are very welcome. So, please to continue.
Anyone else with a question on that chapter?
So no more questions? We can be going having holiday?
No! We'll move on, chapter seven. Do you have one for seven?
He very bossy, you know, is he not? Very bossy fellow, have you noticed? *(Laughter.)*
We going to get him. However, please to continue.

I just wanted to know a little bit more about a Monadic Being.
Is the Divine Spark of who you Be. That is it. It is the aspect of you that is part of the One, the whole, God, whatever terminology. It is that little piece of the God figure that has your name on it. It is who you Be. However, it does not have your current name on it because that is simply a kind of a personality you having for this lifetime. It has your sound. It has your colour. It has your Essence. Is the Essence of who you Be.
Mmm.
Pure Spirit and we mean pure. Your Monadic Being got no kind of a disease within it, no crankiness, no anger, no kind of energy of such. Is pure Love, pure Light. Do you see?
Yes. Thank you.
Thank you very much. What were you going to say?

So, the Monadic Being, Monadic body, Being is that the right term for it?
The Monadic Being exists upon the Monadic plane of

consciousness.

So, the Monadic Being is, as the DNA represents the physical structure composition of the physical body, the Monadic Being represents that spiritual?

Spiritual DNA, that is exactly the situation.

So, the Monadic Being is like the spiritual DNA imprint, whereas the DNA represents the physical structure.

That is so. 'As above, so below.' Whatever, you got here you got there. Whatever you got there, you trying to create here. So your Monad, the Monadic Being, your Essence, whatever term you care to be using is the blueprint in pure Light of who you Be and therefore includes within it all of your potentiality of Being perfect. Not what you got to overcome, that is the soul's purpose. This is what you already got as perfect within you available to you to experience. Again, whole new situation of a book about it; lot of information to be given about that. You only in your world got a little tiny piece of the situation, you know. Actually, very good job because if you had it all, do you know what you be doing? You be blowing up your planet! You already got enough problems as it is! So, please to continue, does this answer your question?

Yes.

Thank you very much. Very good question actually; sometimes you bit bossy but you thinking very quick. Good idea! *(Laughter.)*

Indeed.

Please to continue.

John, this may be a bit out of context but I attend a meeting and we are told that we are God. My concept is that I am part of God but I am not God. I am part of God. When my time comes my closeness to God becomes nearer and nearer until I am really part of God. Now, am I right off the ball here?

Not at all. Is the same situation. Your Monadic Being is that part of your God that is you, do you see?
Yes.
It is part of All That Is and it has chosen to experience, not simply matter but that is the one that we dealing with in this Earth plane. So, that part of you is God, your Monadic Being is God, pure and simple. Not a part of it, it is because All That Is is made up of these Monadic Beings bobbing about the place, do you see?
Yes.
Now, at a physical level, you do not know your Monadic Being. You take a physical form and then you got to make the journey back to being purely spirit because that is what you chosen to do. Not because you being punished but as part of your evolution. Do you see?
Yes.
So the part of you that is here is a part of God *in becoming*. You are striving to reach that pure aspect of who you are that is God because it is pure Spirit and pure Spirit is your God. Do you see?
Yes.

So each lifetime you working upon it to come closer, closer, closer so you do not have to b e returning; so that you are then pure Spirit. You are God. However, you got to do lot of things because you are creating this Karma energy. Obviously you having a better time being in your material world than you do in your spiritual world, else you would not keep coming back again. Does this clarify for you?
Thank you very much, John.
You are most welcome. Do you have another question?

OK, next chapter then. Chapter eight now, Karma.
Oh well then, you not going to have any questions about Karma, are you? *(Laughter.)* You understand it all very perfectly, do you see?
I have a question about Karma. The one I have is probably off track for this actual book. I have the resurrection, soul and Karma.
You have not read all of the final chapter.
No. That's what Tony said.
Have another look at it. Then you'll have lot of questions but not the one you particularly asking.

I have one more. Why is it we get a rainbow of colours across the sky and not horizontally down?
If you read your chapter on colour, you will notice it says that energy comes in at a tangent when it is being seeded, when it is new. Do you recall this? Do you all recall this comment about it? Well, you know, two reasons. Your Earth is a circular object – unless of course you believe it is a square object. Because of the curve of the Earth, from a purely physical situation, you going to see the Light as it bends around your planet, in your rainbow situation, as a arc. However, the reality of the situation is, that because you having Light seeded to your planet all of the time, it is only when you been having your rain and your sun together you can see that the energy is actually coming in. Now, even more important, you never find the ending of your rainbow, do you? Do you know why?
No.
Because that energy being seeded all around the place all of the time. If you were to find it, you be falling off your planet. Do you see? Does this clarify for you?
Yes. It's a good question.
Is a very good question. Is not finished. However, is a very

good question.

Can I ask another one about Karma? I've always wondered what happens Karmically to suicide people.
Nothing.
No, in regards to everybody else around them. The question I might want to ask more about, is it created in their plan when they come, in the human world? Is suicide a plan, a spiritual plan as well?
Suicide is always a spiritual plan.
So it is created in the plan?
How can it not be? It is one option out of many options. For example, you see your suicide as someone who deliberately, consciously says, "I going to be doing this to my physical body so I not awake any longer. I finished with this lifetime."
Mmm.
Well there are many forms of suicide. What about a individual who knows that once they drunk certain amount of substance, their faculties totally out of alignment? They climb into their vehicle and they die because they make a misjudgement. That is suicide, do you see?
Oh, OK.

So when we say to you nothing, suicide has been narrowly defined as those, only those, who say, "I going to end my life in this manner now." If you know something is harmful, specifically harmful to you as a individual, not generally, specifically and you persist in continuing with it, you are choosing to take your own life over a period of time. It is still suicide. Do you see?
Mmm.

Now, every plan for life contains within it points of, you would say, escape clause. If you done everything, you can go at this time, do you see? So you got these points. At some point you may leave and you may choose to do so through suicide. In this situation, you climbing aboard one of your aeroplane. You know is going to crash but you climbing aboard it because you finished. It's the end of your life situation. Those who take their lives, before they incarnate, the ones who are successful about it consciously, have already planned it with all those involved before they began. What we saying to you is not simply confine it to those. There lot of different ways of committing this suicide. Do you see?

So, what I'm hearing is that the soul that decides to incarnate, goes through the period of conception and then doesn't complete the process of evolution within the womb, through miscarriage or whatever, stillborn, that soul has committed suicide?

That is so. If you look at it, take away the emotion of the word, suicide literally means to take the life.
Take your own life.
That is so. A soul that is stillborn has chosen to take away the life, the physical life, because it has completed its journey. It is not a judgment. Your Church judges this as a negative situation. It is not a negative situation. It is evolution, do you see? All those who are connected to that one, grow and develop as a consequence. It is a gift, do you see?
Oh, I see.
It is a gift.
Absolutely.

Is that sometimes brought about in the initial stages to be able to teach whoever it affects?
That is so. Those who are affected already contracted for

that experience so there is a mutual exchange of energy. There is a gift from the one who is suiciding to those about the place to whom they are connected. It is a gift of love, do you see?

Yes, thank you.

Unfortunately, here is your judgement; your Church judges this as a negative, a crime against God. Well, you know, if you think about it, what your Church is saying is that an individual who takes their own life is more powerful than your God. If your God did not intend this situation, would not occur.

No.

What they are saying is that the individual will is more powerful than the Will of God. Well, what a interesting kind of a faith to be preaching, do you see?

Very good!

We try to be very good, you know.

Oh, sorry. It's just made it easier to understand for me.

That is good because that is what we trying to do. Please to continue.

I think that clarity too will help a lot of people at this time. There seems to be a lot of incidents of young people deciding to take their life. And there's no answer for that. I think that will help them.

Because there is no physical answer. For many of them is because the energy of your Earth plane has become so very dense that they cannot fulfil their mission. However, in taking their lives they activate those they are leaving behind to fulfil theirs.

Yes. Indeed.

Is a very powerful gift of Love. And those who judge it have no understanding of it.

It's similar, there's no answer for cot deaths as well, in this

physical realm.
Because is the same situation, do you see?

OK, onwards. Chapter 9 and 10
I have a question about intent and Karma. How is this
recognised? If you're married and you love your spouse
unconditionally, however you choose to experience
someone else, someone else's body, whether your gender
or another. Your intent is purely for you. You feel no malice
in your intent. How is this dealt with Karmically? Or is it the
individual's belief system and how they deal with it for
themselves?
Well, you know, first of all, you asked how is it justified?
Yes, probably, I did.
Subconsciously there is a belief within you, otherwise you
would not ask for it to be justified from the perspective of
Karma and intent. You would ask for it to be explained. Do
you see?
When I say how is this recognised it's the same as asking
for it to be explained.
Is not. Nothing is justified spiritually. Nothing.
And Karmically?
Nothing is justified because in order to justify you are
attaching to it as being inappropriate. Spiritually, everything
is appropriate as a part of learning.
Yes.
So nothing is justified. If you got to justify something, you
got a judgement about it. If you got a judgement about it,
somewhere within you there is a belief contrary to what it is
you are trying to justify.
Yes.
In the example, perhaps we can explain it this way, you
have given. You are with a partner you love unconditionally.
You choose to have an experience with another individual.

Karma will be determined by your intent. Your intent will either be based upon a full understanding of your relationship itself, for example, you and your partner may love each other unconditionally and have no difficulty with either of you having other relationships; therefore there is no harm, do you see?
Yes.

However, if you got a relationship where you love your partner unconditionally, you feel attraction for another individual and you know your partner is going to be harmed by what you do, we would ask you to question the unconditional aspect of your love. We would ask you to ask what is your intent because you are going to step into a situation, which is going to create harm, therefore why? Do you see?
In every situation it is the individual's intent with regard to what it is they are going to do; not their justification, not the rationalisation, *the intent* that will determine whether there is Karma or otherwise. Not the moral standard of your society because the moral standard changes according to what is happening about the place.
Yes. Yes.
Ultimately it is the individual's intent. If that individual says, "I love my partner. However, I wish to experience this. I know it will hurt my partner but I do not care. " There is Karma. If you unconditionally love your partner, you will say to this one, "This is how I am feeling. This is what I wish to be doing." You have been honest about your intent. Do you see?
Yes.
It is the integrity of the intent that denotes whether it is a Karmic situation or not. Does that answer for you?
Yes.

Thank you very much. You quite accurate, a lot more about it. We could be writing forty-five of your books about the whole situation, you know.
(Laughter.) I'm sure

Is there another question?
I have one. My first question is, is there a technique? How can you look at your interpretation or misperception that is being sent down to you?
You cannot.
You cannot?
Do you know why?
Because that's the learning?
Exactly because if you have a technique to avoid it, well, what the dickens you got a physical body for?
I meant more to look at it but it will come through your belief, perception etc.
Exactly because it is the emotional, mental turmoil that is activated that will create the situation where you got to question, do you see?

Yes. How do you know if you've purified your soul energy? Or is that another book?
That depends if you're breathing or not. (Laughter.)
If you purified your soul energy, you're quite accurate is a whole book about it, however, simple short answer you not going to be here.
Mmm.
But then Jesus was in contact with his Monad.
However, He was not purified soul energy until His crucifixion.
Yes. OK.
Do you see? Because during the intervening period, He was activated so, He knew He got to go about doing this

kind of a situation, was very clever fellow, you know. When it came to the point of His ministering to others, talking, sharing, preaching about the place, He was still wrestling with His own soul completion. So, He was purifying it. The purification was denoted by the Crucifixion itself. The feeling is that you in total darkness and you cannot any longer sustain life in that form so you got to leave that body. That body is impregnated with all of the energy of the soul and all of the energy of the lessons of the soul. Once you cleared it that body is no longer required. You may return to be doing work for other people but you got to have another physical body to do it.

And so another soul?
No soul. What you do you come in your Light Body, your capital P personality within a physical form. You gather a physical form around you but you not attaching to it. The soul is the point of attachment to the physical. When it's gone, you can occupy a physical body that you created, (you not going to take it from anybody else or otherwise you got a problem) do what you got to be doing. Then you step out of it. It collapses to the ground and is all finished. Do you see?
Mmm.
Does this clarify?

So when you break away your soul it's the same thing? That's the purification?
When the soul is shattered, that is the purification, that is so. Until that moment of the shattering of the soul energy, you are in the process of the purification. Do you see?
Yes, thank you.
You very welcome. You lot better now are you not?
Heaps better.

Indeed very good. We not going to say any more about what is coming however.

We're not doing the next one.

Well, you know, we got to tell you, you got a wonderful illusion about it. Is there another question or have you finished all your questioning?

I'd like to ask. I'm not sure if this is appropriate. When I got to the end it's like we started at one, belief and belief system and got through to ten, Will to Good, and then it's moving back the other way. We bring it back the other way. That's my understanding.

That is so.

So I was trying to clarify this teaching for myself. I liken it to when I was doing Tai Chi or Ch'I Anau. To me it's an invocation and evocation of energy by using the breath and movement of the body, crossing from left to right. I found the slower the movement and the breathing, the deeper the energy. Then it got to the stage of a turning and dispersing of that energy with power. When using a form like this the sense of moving through Time and Space is in flow. Your day happens as right time, right place.

During the time of doing Tai Chi is when I started to receive symbols. The first symbol I have for me almost encapsulates this teaching. It's like all these words in this whole book are in a symbol, which for me is a trigger. I'm not sure what the question is I'm trying to ask but I guess a clarity on movement and symbolism; where they fit in this teaching.

Very long question!

And actually another book!

Oh, OK. So, we'll forget that one?

No because the point is do not be forgetting the question is very important. The point is, in this particular volume, we

trying to give to you, if you will, a understanding of a philosophy, a foundation. If you got that then your concrete mind and your emotional body will allow you to explore in other areas because you got something of a kind of a security stage to be standing upon. Do you see?
Yes.
Then you can move into lot more about sound and key and pitch and tone and all this kind of a thing; and Karma and different kinds of a energy. You can be talking about your symbols. All of these are detailed aspects of this general presentation of the philosophy. Movement is very significant. Breathing is most significant. That in itself is a movement and a rhythm. If your breathing is not in rhythm, the movement of it creates disease. So a lot of information of this kind of a nature is still to be presented because that is about healing. That is about using your philosophy symbolically to create wholeness: to create and build your Light body because that is what you doing. Do you see?
Yes.

When the Temple was shattered, what was shattered was not a physical building somewhere about the place. What was shattered were your Light Bodies. You are in the process of rebuilding them so you do not have to have a physical form at any further point in time. We already talked about it to these two individuals. You can put that into the book, so thank you for your question. That is what ascension is. It is not stepping out of your body, picking it up, carrying it with you somewhere else to be using it. It is creating your Light body because then you can go anywhere, be anywhere, do anything. That is being one with your God.
So do you have any other question? Does this clarify little bit for you?
Yes, thanks.

Do you have a question?
Or have we finished answering all of your questions we can now be going for holiday?
Yes, you can do that.
Very good. We need to be having a holiday because we going to be very busy, do you see?
We thank you all for your time and your energy. We thank you all for your willingness to be part of what we been doing; for your generosity in sharing your questioning. We would ask you to continue to ponder upon what we presented because then you can be a part of the next question/ answer situation, do you see?
Yes.
And then we can all be having a very good time! We thank you all.
Thank you, John.
Go with our blessing and our love until we meet again.
For I am John.

Notes.